GRACE
Abounds

Since I have been speaking at the Anaheim Congress from almost the beginning, I can truthfully say that Sr. Edith has been the shining light who has illuminated it for many of those years—both personally and professionally. Her stellar and passionate keynotes, gathered beautifully here, will inspire and educate us for years to come!

Richard Rohr, O.F.M.
Center for Action and Contemplation

This moving and poetic book is all about grace, another name for God's effective love at work in our lives. And no one is more credible to write it than Edith Prendergast. I say this because Edith herself has been such a means of grace not only to the Los Angeles Archdiocese but to the American Catholic community, especially through the famous Religious Education Congress that she has organized these many years. This book comes from the heart of a great woman with a deep Catholic faith. Sit back and treat yourself!

Thomas H. Groome
Professor of Theology and Religious Education
Boston College

Grace Abounds delightfully dusts off the true essentials of the spiritual life. Weaving poetry, scripture, and theology together with meaningful stories and lessons, Edith Prendergast enables us not only to be more deeply grateful for all we already have, but also opens us up to the vast possibilities still there for us in our relationship with God. Truly nourishing.

Robert J. Wicks
Author of *Prayerfulness*

Educators and church ministers of every kind will find in these pages inspiration and perspective to enrich their souls and enliven their work. Sr. Edith Prendergast, a talented religious educator and a visionary leader, has a graceful way of weaving together poetry, wisdom, and popular culture for the good of the reader and the flourishing of ministries.

Michael P. Horan
Professor of Theological Studies
Loyola Marymount University

Sr. Edith Prendergast touches our hearts and souls with her profound insights. What a valuable book to anchor us in God's presence!

Anne Bryan Smollin
Author of *Live, Laugh, and Be Blessed*

GRACE *Abounds*

A CALL TO AWAKEN AND RENEW YOUR FAITH

EDITH PRENDERGAST, R.S.C.

ave maria press AMP notre dame, indiana

Additional acknowledgments are found on page 111, which is a continuation of this copyright page.

Founded in 1865, Ave Maria Press is a ministry of the Indiana Province of Holy Cross.

www.avemariapress.com

ISBN-10 1-59471-259-X   ISBN-13 978-1-59471-259-3

Cover and text design by Andy Wagoner.

Printed and bound in the United States of America.

Library of Congress Cataloging-in-Publication Data

Prendergast, Edith.
  Grace abounds : a call to awaken and renew your faith / Edith Prendergast.
    p. cm.
  ISBN-13: 978-1-59471-259-3 (pbk.)
  ISBN-10: 1-59471-259-X (pbk.)
  1. Christian life--Catholic authors. I. Title.
  BX2350.3.P75 2011
  248.4'82--dc22

                                    2010041751

I graciously dedicate *Grace Abounds* to
the many thousands of parish ministers
who have graced me in abundance.
Their presence, passion for ministry,
and participation in so many
Archdiocesan Religious Education Congresses
has inspired, stretched, and encouraged me.
I am grateful to all
who have companioned me on the journey
and who have taught me to discover God's presence
in the simple and the profound.
In particular, I am grateful for the
poets and prophets who have shaped my thoughts
and inspired my words.
My heartfelt thanks to
my parents Catherine and Richard,
Cardinal Roger Mahony,
the staff of the Office of Religious Education,
The Religious Sisters of Charity,
Monsignor Lloyd Torgerson,
Dr. Michael Downey,
family and friends.
Their support and unwavering trust
is both gift and blessing.

CONTENTS

FOREWORD

For nearly a quarter century, Sister Edith Prendergast, R.S.C., has served as the Director of the Office of Religious Education in the Archdiocese of Los Angeles. In addition to her faithful service in assuring that our religious education and faith formation programs are of the highest quality, Sister Edith has been responsible for the Los Angeles Religious Education Congress, a gathering of nearly 40,000, held annually at the Anaheim Convention Center. Representing dozens of countries around the world, participants come together for four days of what has come to be known worldwide simply as "Congress." Far more than a conference on methods of catechetical instruction, Congress is a multi-generational, multi-cultural Catholic *event* that provides an opportunity for a deeper immersion in the riches of our living faith tradition. Clergy, religious, and lay faithful participate in Congress in the hope of being nourished and sustained in their faith as they pray together, celebrate the Eucharist and the sacrament of Reconciliation, listen attentively to theologians, pastors, and practitioners, lift their voices in songs of praise and thanksgiving, stroll through a great exhibition hall chock full of the finest in Catholic books, worship aids, and catechetical materials, and get together with old friends and make new ones. The spirit of Congress is difficult to describe, in much the same way that our efforts to pin down a description of the Holy Spirit usually fall short. But it is palpable.

Year by year, it is Sister Edith who charts the course and sets the tone of Congress by addressing the gathered assembly at the opening morning prayer service. Taking up the Congress theme inspired by the Sunday readings of Congress weekend, Sister Edith demonstrates that her skills as a catechist are second to none. Like any true teacher in the faith, she knows that Christ's message is not best conveyed in concept. She invites her listeners to hear the Scriptures afresh, to hark to the words of the prophets and the poets, to redouble their efforts to be and become a sign of reconciliation and peace in the Church and the wider world.

After years of gentle prodding by friends, colleagues, and publishers, Sister Edith has finally agreed to gather together some of her Congress opening talks. It is a singular delight for me to know that these words of wisdom and discernment, first spoken in the faith-filled assembly of the Los Angeles Religious Education Congress, will now reach the eyes, ears, and hearts of so many more of God's holy people who are longing for an encouraging word.

His Eminence Cardinal Roger Mahony
Archbishop of Los Angeles

PREFACE

Waterford. The legendary glass first crafted in the Irish city of the same name. A hallmark of the heritage of a people, Waterford is a timeless gift, given and received from generation to generation. It is clear. Crystal. Every careful cut of it allows the light streaming through to glisten as the eye beholds hues of shimmering pastels. It is warm to the touch. When we tap it gently or circle 'round the lip of the goblet with our fingertip, soothing tones echo out of the very openness of it. The wordless echo springs from the deeps of it, humming in the ear and drawing the eye to look again, and again, and yet again upon a beauty at once so clear and complex, strong and so fragile. In a moment, or in a year's time, Waterford lets the light pour through it as if for the very first time. The light that never changes. The light that is never twice the same.

Waterford. The birthplace of Sister Edith Prendergast, R.S.C. Even though she has been in Los Angeles for most of her religious life, the ways of Waterford run like a deep well in her. I count myself one among so many who have been refreshed by her presence, her care, her spark, and her spunk.

Even though Edith and I have been friends and colleagues for nearly thirty years, I do not know much about her experiences in Waterford in the early years. What I do know is that she attributes her vocation to religious life to her father. Witness to her father's extraordinary generosity toward those less fortunate than his own family, this Prendergast girl found her heart's home in the Religious Sisters of Charity in Dublin, founded there by Mary Aikenhead in 1815 for the purpose of meeting the needs of those who suffer because of poverty, illness, and ignorance. For thirty-seven years Sister Edith has made her home in the Archdiocese of Los Angeles, impelled by the inspiration of her religious congregation, *Caritas Christi urget nos*, the love of Christ urges us on (2 Cor 5:14).

We in the Archdiocese of Los Angeles, and well beyond, have come to know her as a woman of the Church, teacher, catechist, administrator, wise guide, and spiritual director. Above all, she is a woman whose efforts for the benefit of so many are beyond calculation. But when it comes to care, courage, and compassion, Edith never learned her numbers; she never learned to count. And then there are the other small acts of kindness done quietly and in secret, known only to those who have received of the gift of her generosity. She is a sister to us all, truly a daughter of Mary Aikenhead, truly her father's daughter.

Year after year, Sister Edith addresses those gathered at the Los Angeles Religious Education Congress in the opening morning prayer service. The lights are bright, listeners many, applause long. What the crowds do not know is just how long, how much care, how much prayer it takes to craft one of these Congress addresses. Long before the annual gathering, in consultation with the staff of the Office of Religious Education, a theme for Congress is chosen in accord with the Gospel for the Sunday of Congress weekend. Then, among so many other pressing duties, Edith takes up the discipline of allowing the words of the Congress theme and the Gospel for that Sunday to "drop down" in her, as she puts it.

From time to time she invites me to her office to "chat me up" or have a little "prayer talk." Quietly she rehearses this or that part of her address, months before Congress. She asks my thoughts. She jots down a note here and there. She takes from me what is helpful, and leaves the rest aside. I come away from the quiet refreshed by the lilt in her delivery, by the lines from poets I've never read, by the words of scripture heard so often I cannot count, but which I daily fail to live. Her words, her presence, quicken in me a faith that is hope.

Like Waterford, each piece in this collection is crafted with impeccable skill and consummate care. Each one is clear, crystal clear, allowing the light who is Christ to pierce it through and through. The beauty of that light is all the more, not less, because of the pastels both subtle and sparkling which are to be discerned in the lines of the likes of Mary Oliver and John Chrysostom, John O'Donoghue and Catherine of Genoa, Jessica Powers and Anselm, George Herbert and Simone Weil. All chime in on the great doxology to which Edith invites us. Each time the words ring true. Every time they are new because they echo a timeless Word. The Word beneath and beyond all words, the Word Edith seeks and stretches to speak, is the Word above all speaking whose name above all names is love (1 Jn 4:8).

This love is the very light and life of God given as gift. But the gift comes only to those who know how to receive. The gift comes in the hollow of our hearts, hallowing even our broken-ness, emptiness, weakness, and darkness. Over and over, Edith's discerning eye opens ours to see that nothing, even and especially the hardness of our own hearts, is outside the embrace of grace that finds a way, or makes a way, for light to stream through to the deeps of us. Then, by the light coming out of the two eyes of us, we see anew as if for the first time. And we know firsthand that it is in the dark times that the eye begins to see. The blind shall see. The lame shall leap. The poor shall eat and have their fill. A time will come for singing. And the words of the song are ones we know, but too often forget. And then forget that we have forgot-ten. From her early days in Waterford until now, Edith has helped us remember the lines by whispering in lilting tones: The love of Christ urges us on.

In the days of the early Desert Fathers, a monk would seek advice from the Abbot by saying: "Father, give me a word." For nearly twenty-five years I have been among those gathered for Edith's opening talks at Congress with thousands from lands near and far, whose hearts seem to whispering: "Mother, give us a word." Citing the poet David Whyte, Edith reminds us: "One good word is bread for a thousand." Now the good word echoes beyond Sister Edith's listeners to all who take up this book and read.

Michael Downey

1

AWAKE TO GRACE

The grace bestowed on us in Christ Jesus before time began,
[is] now made manifest through the appearance of our savior.

2 Timothy 1:9–10

Every poet knows what every good theologian affirms: that "Every breath we draw is a gift of His love and every moment of existence is a grace!" (Thomas Merton). But are we awake to grace? Have we arisen from our sleep and come out of the dark night of our blindness? Do we walk in the daylight of simplicity and surprise? Do we delight in the favor of God that is renewed every day, the all-pervasive presence of the One who graces us?

From the beginning of time, the grace of God has been woven into the fabric of our universe, into the lives of all humanity. As Genesis proclaimed: "God looked at everything he had made, and he found it very good" (Gn 1:31). Indeed, we can affirm that "earth is crammed with heaven and every common bush is afire with God." When God called Abraham, God said: "Through you the nations of the earth will be blessed." The love of God is universal, but also specific. From that moment forward, we, too, have been drawn into the story of God's determination to bless humanity. The pilgrim People of God knew that they were borne up by grace in holiness and faithfulness.

The ultimate and infinite display of grace, present as promise and hope in the Hebrew scriptures, was revealed in the life of Jesus. Jesus describes a world overflowing with God's grace: where the sun shines on people, good and bad; where birds gather seeds gratis, neither plowing nor harvesting to gain them; where untended wildflowers burst into bloom on rocky hills. The grace of God poured out in Jesus was what the poet John O'Donohue called "the permanent climate of divine kindness." It has remained among us, even within reach of our senses. We find it available in the experience of beauty, or empowerment, or any good beyond ourselves.

With Jesus came the revelation that God is essentially a God of grace and compassion, that God is one who understands our fears and who will persistently seek access to our hearts. His graciousness will eventually take sufficient hold on us to make us more and more like him.

The great news is that Jesus didn't take this grace with him when he ascended. Rather, he poured it forth in our hearts by the Holy Spirit who wraps us in his love. He gifts us with his presence, veiled in bread and wine, and saves us by grace. It is a gift overflowing in a Christ-drenched universe.

This is the gifted awareness that mystics share with us. We have been graced in our history with many great spiritual teachers whose insights can guide us. Francis of Assisi amazed his companions because he lived as if he were already in paradise. Brother Lawrence of the Resurrection gazed at a barren tree and watched it swell with life before his eyes. Gazing out the window of his hermitage, Thomas Merton wrote, "The great work of the sunrise again today. The awful solemnity of it. The sacredness."

God shows God's self everywhere, in the bits and pieces of every day, but so often we don't see it. We miss the presence, we miss the cue. We fail to locate God in the ordinary raw experiences of our lives and ministry.

Famed preacher-poet Edwin Markham expresses well our condition in his poem "How the Great Guest Came." He writes,

Conrad sighed as the world turned gray:
"Why is it, Lord, that your feet delay?
Did you forget that this was the day?"
Then soft in the silence a voice he heard,
"Lift up your heart, for I have kept my word.
Three times I came to your friendly door;
Three times my shadow was on your floor.
I was a beggar with the bruised feet;
I was the woman you gave to eat;
I was the child on the homeless street!"

Grace can be unnoticed or it can be refused. We become so mesmerized with external voices and the expectations of others that we bury the inner voice of God's word under a mound of preoccupation. The writer Henry Ward Beecher reveals how we can miss this presence:

There are joys which long to be ours. God sends ten thousand truths which come about like birds seeking inlet, but we are shut up to them, and so they bring us nothing, but sit and sing awhile upon the roof and then fly away.

We are blind to the gift of grace or deaf to the visitation. Instead of fully participating in the great adventure of life, we fall asleep. The price of falling asleep can be astounding. We forget our true vocation in life: the call to love, to care, to connect, and to share with others. We may not wake up until we die.

Still, God is always seeking to draw us from the ordinary into mystery and we are often too busy to notice. We are in a great hurry, not because our lives are so full, though that is always the way we account for our hurriedness, but because we are so empty.

Etty Hillesum, a young Dutch-Jewish woman who died in Auschwitz, wrote:

> There is a really deep well inside of us. And in it dwells God. Sometimes, I am there too. But more often stones and grit block the well, and God is buried beneath. Then God must be dug out again.

Who, then, will teach us to dig deeply, to savor each moment and understand the blessedness of the "present," the "now"? To be awake to grace is to remain anchored in God's presence even in the midst of the outburst of confusion and anxiety that can engulf our days.

We are summoned to assume a spirit of watchfulness. St. Therese of Lisieux describes this spirit of watchfulness as "an upward leap of the heart, an untroubled glance toward heaven, a cry of gratitude and love which I utter from the depth of sorrow as well as from the height of joy." We need only to glance in God's direction from time to time. If we trust in the intimacy of God's loving presence, then we need only to pay attention.

We struggle with all kinds of fears and insecurities: fear of criticism, fear of our inadequacies and our failures. Yet the great paradox of our lives is that these flaws and defects are the very crevices through which grace finds entrance. As St. Paul reminds us, "My grace is sufficient for you, for power is made perfect in weakness" (2 Cor 12:9). Indeed, even imperfection can be a grace if it binds us both to God and to humanity, and leads us to compassion for ourselves and our community.

Grace hits us when we are in great pain or restlessness. It hits us when we meander through a gloomy valley of a purposeless and empty life. It strikes us when, year after year, the longed-for perfection does not surface, when the old impulses remain with us as they have for decades, when anguish destroys all joy and courage.

I came across a narrative of such a story in the memoirs of Peter Greave, author of *The Seventh Gate*. Peter tells of his experience of contracting leprosy while stationed in India. He goes on to relate how he returned to England. He took up residence at a compound run by Anglican nuns. As his eyesight deteriorated into partial blindness and his body struggled to adapt to partial paralysis, his frustration and bitterness grew as he grappled with his inability to work and his increasing sense of alienation from society. Eventually, he found himself contemplating suicide as his inner despair continued to deepen and threatened to engulf his spirit. He told of his efforts to escape the compound and how he always found himself blocked as he grew to realize how limited his options really were.

One morning, he arose for a morning stroll through the grounds and was drawn by a quiet buzz coming from the small chapel where the sisters were in prayer. Intrigued by their prayer, he tells of entering the chapel to find its interior walls inscribed with all the names of those people for whom the sisters were committed to care. It was their custom to pray daily for their charges. In a moment of wonder, Peter recognized his own name among the many on the wall, and this simple recognition transformed his life. He felt his inner despair collapse as wholeness returned. He felt included . . . connected . . . accepted. He was graced.

In times of fear, anxiety, and disillusionment, grace beckons us to put our trust in God, who, according to the Spanish poet Antonio Machado, "makes white combs and sweet honey from our old failures." Indeed, terror and pain become opportunities for grace, calling us to greatness and beckoning us to stretch our perspective.

When we are tempted to fall prey to fear and discouragement, it might be helpful to hear the words of the Indian poet Rabindranath Tagore:

> I thought that my voyage had come to its end
> at the last limits of my power
> —that the path before me was closed . . .
> But I find that . . . when old words die out
>   on the tongue,
> new melodies break forth from the heart;
> and where old tracks are lost,
> new country is revealed with its wonders.

We know that grace is personally transformative; but at the same time, it makes us agents of transformation for others. God's extravagant love draws our hearts to the grace of new possibilities, fills us with a new kind of freedom and hope, and challenges us to just and right relationships. The grace of God operates at a profound level in our compassionate response to those in need, especially to the poor. So often the direction of our lives is changed by our encounter with a person in need. To be awake to grace is to be prophetically involved with the plight of our global community.

When we experience uncertainty, disappointment, poverty, war, or terror, we need to be disciples who will give vision and hope. Jesus was such a gracious visionary. He opened up eyes to see with new perspectives, opened ears to hear afresh. He delighted in giving freedom to those who were demon-possessed and to all who were in any way burdened. His presence brought forth life, and the ways in which he went about his daily ministry spoke of care and compassion.

But there is a cost to this kind of discipleship. Dietrich Bonhoeffer, a Lutheran pastor who was imprisoned and put to death by the Nazis for his resistance, makes the marvelous distinction between "cheap grace" and "costly grace." "Cheap grace is grace without discipleship, grace without the Cross, and grace without Jesus Christ." It is an intellectual assent, but requires no moral courage. On the other hand, "costly grace" is the grace of discipleship, of truly following the way of Jesus Christ—a way that leads first to the cross before it leads to the resurrection.

Bonhoeffer chose "costly grace." What about us? What about our ministry, our relationships, our choices? We all encounter the cross in one way or another in our lives and in our ministries. Grace is God's gift to wake us up and empower us as disciples. It is grace that summons us to ask the hard questions: How do we build a world of harmony? Of justice and peace? How do we stand in solidarity with those who have lost much? A number of years ago, the Jesuit theologian Jon Sobrino shared some thoughts after a series of serious earthquakes in El Salvador. His reflection, "The Human Family in Face of Disaster," offers some apt wisdom:

> Allowing ourselves to be affected is salvific, because it roots us in truth and allows [us] to transcend the unreality with which we surround ourselves. Allowing yourself to be affected by the disaster can produce solidarity. And so, alongside the ethical obligation to help, appears something deeper and more decisive—the sense of closeness among human beings.
>
> Let us hope that solidarity helps us to rebuild our houses, but above all our people. Let us hope it helps to repair our roads, but above all our ways of walking through this life. Let us

> hope it helps us build our churches, but above
> all the people of God.
> May such solidarity bring hope to this
> people.

Called to be disciples of Jesus, we must invest in a community that is bigger than any one of us. When we turn inward and focus only on our own problems, we cut ourselves off from the source of our strength. The work of the disciple must go on. We must break new ground, but there is a cost to discipleship. It requires a commitment, one that we are invited to over and over again.

Grace strengthens us for the journey. Having fed upon the body and blood of Christ, we flow from our sanctuaries to flood our neighborhoods, our families, and workplaces with Christ's presence in our hearts. Annie Dillard suggests that "being empty and hollow, you can catch grace as a person holds a cup under a waterfall." May we catch grace and may we greet one another with great hope and compassion, forgiveness, and empowerment as the early Christians did when they bid each other "grace be upon you." May grace abound more in us.

2

INCREDIBLE ABUNDANCE

God's love is so immense, so tender, so dazzling with joy
that most of us have only felt the hem of it.

Sue Monk Kidd

The story of God's incredible abundance is the Christian story
deeply rooted in the Jewish tradition. It is the saga of the creative,
incredible Giver of Life shining through the people, the memo-
ries, the rituals, the poetry of our faith tradition, and of our lives
today. It is the sound of what Sue Monk Kidd calls "the one great
echo in the universe . . . God's great confession, 'I love you.'"

God's incredible abundance is overflowing in love and compassion. We need only to pause, to look, to listen. When we do,
we begin to see more than the hem of the garment of God's immense love; we see the whole amazing, multicolored cloak. Mary
Oliver's poetry recounts the breathtaking signs of God's abundance all around us: in nature and the physical world, in the
sights, sounds, and wonder of all creation. She says, "Sometimes I
need only to stand wherever I am to be blessed."

Let us be wide-eyed, quick to recognize the miracles of grace in our lives, the many echoes of a God who longs to give God's self away. Scripture reminds us of the abundance of God's sustaining spirit. Recall that for forty years the refugee nation of Israel received its daily sustenance—manna—dribbling down in the shape of bread, directly, we might say, from God. Then, they entered the promised land where the psalmist exclaimed, "We feast on the rich food of your house; from your delightful stream you give us drink" (Ps 36:9). This is a God who takes to heart our very basic needs; a God who, in Christ, is involved in the very stuff of our lives. Through him, the forces of death and despair are overcome; the stones and grit that block the flow of life are removed. Standing before the tomb of Lazarus, Jesus said, "Roll away the stone." So, too, he says to us, "Let the fresh air flow, let something new happen." How often, in our emptiness, does a gracious hand reach out, lift us up, and set us on a new path? How often, when we are down, does a compassionate voice give us the courage to go on?

This was Johanna's experience. For many years, she struggled with a sense of darkness. She often talked with me about her life as an experience of going through an endless dark tunnel, wondering if she would ever see the light shining again. But through the presence and encouragement of friends who really cared to listen and to hear her pain, she heard the voice of God reminding her, "I am with you." She allowed these words to go deep in her spirit and gradually felt the heavy load lifting. She shared with me how her pace of life changed, no longer carrying a heavy burden, but walking with a light step. She had a sense of God's incredible abundance being poured out on her, lightening her journey. She said, "I did not look back; I was on my way to wholeness."

The promise of Jesus, "I came so that they may have life, and have it more abundantly" (Jn 10:10), shows up not only in Johanna's story, but also powerfully in God's stance toward those in need of forgiveness and of healing—Zaccheus, the woman at the well, the blind Bartimaeus, and so many more. Confronted by human failure, Jesus responds not by condemning, but by exposing wounds to the light and comforting. We, too, have that same need to depend on the wideness of God's mercy and compassionate care. But will we open up our hearts? Will we acknowledge our need for healing? Will we take the necessary steps out of ourselves and into the field of God's mercy?

Recently, I happened to meet Sam at a shopping center. Sam, an eighty-four year old man, was sitting at a coffee table on his own. We exchanged greetings and he invited me to sit down. He seemed anxious to talk and soon was telling me his story. He lived alone, but never really alone, he said, as God was always with him. It hadn't always been that way. He had lived a fairly wayward life, much like St. Augustine. But he felt God's hand reaching out, beckoning him. So a few years ago he decided to become a member of a Presbyterian church where he now serves as a deacon and hospitality minister. This has changed his life. He now has a reason to get up every morning. His life is very full, happy, and content. Our amazing God is always on the lookout to welcome us home. Sam had the courage to step out of himself into the field of God's prodigal love, and it made all the difference.

Indeed, we can affirm with Simone Weil, "Grace fills empty spaces, but it can only enter where there is a void to receive it, and it is grace itself that makes the void." We understand that we are God's people of abundance, not scarcity. Yet talking about abundance may sound foolish, even irresponsible, today. How can there be joy in a job lost? How can there be hope in a relationship gone sour? How can a song ring out from a city in ruin? In the midst of the devastation in Port au Prince, Haiti, after the catastrophic 2010 earthquake, we learned that worshippers gathered on folded metal chairs under bougainvillea and mimosa trees and sang the hymn, "How Great Thou Art." We wonder how someone can sing, smile, or dance amid destruction. It is the paradox of God's presence not only in success and well-being, but also in pain and questioning. God was there in Haiti in each and every face who attended the wounded—in the doctors, the nurses, the rescue workers. God was there in each embrace from every stranger who risked harm to bring relief and save lives. This is God's way, not to keep the darkness away, but to shine a ray of light in the gloom, to sing a melody of trust in the desolation.

When we recognize that the other side of abundance is lack or loss, we must choose to which we will give our energy. Rabbi Harold Kushner says, "If you concentrate on finding what is good in every situation, you will discover that your life will suddenly be filled with gratitude, a feeling that nurtures the soul." When we decide not to focus on what is missing, on the negative, but rather dwell on the abundance already experienced and still present, fears and anxieties slip away. We are immersed in the sheer delight of being alive and vital.

But there are lessons to be gleaned from loss. We learn that when we think we can no longer go on, when everyone else is saying "you're done, it's over," that is when the inner resources buried beneath a façade of self-sufficiency emerge to carry us along. Wendell Berry offers some wisdom. He says, "We pray to be quiet in heart, and eye clear—what we need is here." God wants to breathe fresh hope into our hearts, and we are called to trust in the sentiments expressed in Psalm 30: "At dusk weeping comes for the night; but at dawn there is rejoicing" (Ps 30:6). And as Paul said to the Romans, nothing "will be able to separate us from the love of God in Christ Jesus our Lord" (Rom 8:39). If we live in that expectation, then we will rise each day with the nerve to face the challenges and believe that we will not only survive but will be lifted up; we will walk and run again.

Gratefulness is essential to a contented life. If we are not grateful, then no matter how much we have or possess, we will not be satisfied; we will always be on the lookout for something more. G. K. Chesterton reminds us of the availability of that munificence of God. He writes, "You say grace before meals. All right. But I say grace before a concert and the opera, and grace before the play and the pantomime, and grace before I open a book, and grace before sketching, painting, swimming, fencing, boxing, walking, playing, dancing and grace before I dip the pen in ink." This prayer is an acknowledgement of the many ways we encounter the abundance of God's graciousness in the ordinary.

The world coaches us to store up treasure, to grow our bank accounts, to win, grab, and get. The gospel, on the other hand, invites us to sit in the company of others and to care about their needs, to trust that open-handedness is more powerful than any market. Maybe we can join our prayer to the prayer of the poet George Herbert:

> Thou hast given so much to me,
> Give me one thing more—a grateful heart;
> Not thankful when it pleaseth me,
> As if thy blessings had spare days;
> But such a heart, whose pulse may be,
> Thy praise

What does it mean for us to live inside of our abundance and lead from that center? It means that God's brightness, mercy, and care must sing through us and light up our spirits and our world. Now is the time for us to show the world that there is another way, a way marked by blessing and gratitude, a way sustained by our "yes" to the banquet of life, the eucharistic feast. Now is the time for us to show all the miracle of what God's presence does in our lives and in our world.

"A good person out of the store of goodness in his heart produces good . . . for from the fullness of the heart the mouth speaks" (Lk 6:45). Our task is to help build a society, a community of comfort, joy, and abundance. Let us remember the Buddhist saying, "It is our turn to help the world."

Imagine offering radical gospel hospitality: care for all, care for the earth. Let us imagine peace and nonviolence for ourselves in a world of peace and justice where no mouth is left hungry and the forgotten are embraced. Let us imagine a world of enough for all. Let us imagine touching sadness with a smile. Let us imagine touching discouragement with hope. Embracing this incredible abundance, we trust that it is never too late for God to invigorate and revitalize a person, a church, the world.

3

CLOTHED IN LOVE, SUMMONED BEYOND

God fills my being to the brim
with floods of His immensity.
I drown within a drop of Him
whose sea-bed is infinity.

Jessica Powers

God invites us to sink deeply into the realization that we are
clothed in love and summoned beyond to join Jesus on the Way.
Ravished by God's boundless love poured out in Christ through
the power of the Spirit, we are summoned to reach out, to break
boundaries—to taste what lies beyond. Filled to the brim with
God's love, we are called to let our lives overflow with love into
one another. In a world haunted by terror, this call is more poi-
gnant and urgent than ever before.

Yet through all our trials, Julian of Norwich reminds us that "God is our clothing. In His love, He wraps and holds us. He enfolds us for love and will never let us go. We are wrapped and held in the embrace of God's all-pervasive love for each of us, the love that calls us by name, that makes us precious in God's sight." This is not a fanciful notion, but something at the heart of reality and connected to our everyday lives. It means that within us is a living power, the Holy Spirit, the divine force that turns self-effacing women like Mary and apprehensive men like Peter into apostles who changed the world. It means that in the power of the Spirit we can love as Jesus loved . . . without discrimination, without counting the cost.

There is a story recounted about this love and sacrifice. Elie Wiesel, a young Orthodox Jew and writer who survived the death camps of the Holocaust, tells a magnificent, heartfelt story of bread and sacrifice. Every day, the guards would give the prisoners their one meager meal of bread and some soup. Wiesel remembers so clearly how his father would graciously give half of his bread each day to his small son. This little gesture of care and concern kept Wiesel alive, but his father grew weaker every day and eventually died. Only later did Wiesel come to understand that his father, by sharing his meal, had hastened his own death.

The love of Elie Wiesel's father for his son overflowed from him in the form of bread, and ultimately, in the form of total self-giving—the sacrificial offering of his own life. It is this same sacrificial love that God gives to all God's people, and it is this love that wells up in us, allowing us to love as freely and as generously as Wiesel's father. Therefore, we celebrate God's delight in us and give ourselves to God's gracious desire for us. In the words of Psalm 104, "we are clothed with honor and majesty." Marked with the blueprint of God, we discover our God-given ability to love and to forgive as Jesus loved and forgave. We discover the

freedom we have to make choices, to live as we are intended to
live, to imagine and to shape our world.

The poet Rainer Maria Rilke beautifully articulates the desire
to carry within ourselves the image and likeness of God:

> I want to mirror your immensity,
> I never want to be too weak or too old,
> to bear the heavy lurking image of You.
> Clothed in love, we mirror God.

It seems an incredible task to mirror the immensity of God,
whose "sea-bed is infinity." Yet the Gospel of Matthew asks us,
"If God so clothes the grass of the field, which grows today and
is thrown into the oven tomorrow, will he not much more pro-
vide for you, O you of little faith?" (Mt 6:30). Shielded in the
embrace of a loving God and filled with courage, we can make a
fresh start.

To begin, we can dare to allow God's love to touch us deeply;
to uncover our hidden blemishes, our tired and sagging spiritual
clothes, our demons. Calling upon the Holy Spirit, the Carmelite
poet Jessica Powers bids us to risk this fresh start in "Come, South
Wind":

> I have walked too long with a death's chill in
> the air,
> mourned over trees too long with branches
> bare. . . .
> I am saying to Love who wakens love:
> rise in the south and come!
> Hurry me into the springtime; hustle the
> winter out of my sight . . .
> . . .Then plunge me
> into my leafing and my blossoming . . .

Naked and vulnerable before God, as prodigal sons and daughters, we hear the ever-ancient, yet ever-new, words spoken on our behalf: "Quickly bring the finest robe and put it on him/ [her]; put a ring on his/[her] finger and sandals on his/[her] feet. Take the fattened calf and slaughter it. Then let us celebrate with a feast, because this son/[daughter] of mine was dead, and has come to life again . . . was lost, and has been found" (Lk 15:23–24). When we are lost, God finds us and clothes us with compassion and mercy. We put on new skin; we throw off those clothes that are torn and need mending.

In their place, we put on brand-new garments of love for a God who experienced in our flesh all that we experience. We acknowledge our own inherent goodness—not what we have become on our own, but what God's love has made of us: a new creation. We see dignity in ourselves and others, knowing we are wrapped with God's love and likeness. We draw up fresh love for our brothers and sisters who are images of the living God whom we touch each day in a smile, a phone call, a dinner, or a casual encounter. Would that we might have the insight of Hildegard of Bingen, who on meeting a human being in the streets, would affirm that, "Every creature is a glittering, glistening mirror of divinity."

We read in Luke's gospel that Jesus was "wrapped in swaddling clothes and lying in a manger" (Lk 2:12). God's gift of new life was wrapped in swaddling clothes and given to the world so that the world might know God, know love poured out for all. In baptism, we, too, are wrapped in swaddling clothes of white, clothed with love, and drawn into relationship with God and all of humanity. Our baptism stands as a sign of our commitment to being faithful disciples of Jesus Christ and children of light. We have a responsibility placed upon us by our baptism. God calls us to transform our corner of God's world; to cultivate it into a terrain of justice and peace.

We cannot ignore this call, for all around us are images of the crucified Christ. Too many people live in parts of the world where fear and violence, hunger and death, war and nuclear threats are their daily food. We think, for instance, of Israel and Palestine, Iraq and Afghanistan. We could list many others, remembering those countries where oppressive regimes, military rule, and dictatorial leaders cause distress, want, and privation for their own people. And, so, we have to ask over and over again: What does our love have to say to the world?

The prophet Isaiah says, "God has clothed me with a robe of salvation, and wrapped me in a mantle of justice" (Is 61:10). Now it is our turn to wrap others in a mantle of justice, to give hope even in face of the inevitable pain and distress that comes from terrorist activities and conflicts that tear apart the fabric of our lives and relationships. We do well, also, to remember that we ourselves contribute to violence and terrorism in so far as we, in our ordinary lives in community and ministry, act in anger or fail to forgive. Our small expressions of selfishness and our petty acts of spitefulness contribute to the evil that explodes in the horrendous actions we witness in our world today. Conversely, every act of ours that is kind, forgiving, and generous flows out and blooms in the great experiences of peace and valor that equally give a name to our world.

Often we are at a loss to know how to heal the hurts and hungers all around us, yet we know that we must be involved and engaged in the agony of the world. Jesus taught us that love is stronger than hate and that forgiveness is greater than revenge. However, there is a painful price for assuming this stance. Often there are those who ridicule us for turning the other cheek. They want to demand the pound of flesh; love and forgiveness are not high on their radar. Yet we must not waver. In the words of the General Council of my community, the Religious Sisters of Charity, we are called to "follow the poor Christ who knew suffering, pain, and rejection and whose loving surrender redeemed our broken world." We will find that our love actually matures and deepens as we forget ourselves for awhile and reach out in care and compassion for the other. God's desire for our well-being calls us to be involved in a world bigger than our own puny confines. A love that is not for more than itself will stagnate and die. Consequently, we must ask ourselves some serious questions:

- Do our programs and processes mediate healing, compassion, and unity?
- Who is in and who is out of our circles of inclusion?
- Do we forgive ourselves and others—especially those who seem least deserving of forgiveness?

Ultimately, we must ask ourselves: Are we using the power that lies within us? The *Los Angeles Times* reported the story of a woman who certainly used the power within her. At age eighty-one, Mary McAnena met a homeless young woman who was using her fingers to eat pork and beans from a can. She took the woman in, gave her keys to her home, and cared for her for several weeks as she tried to find her a job. This experience inspired Mary to launch a program to feed the hungry, which now serves more than a hundred people a day. One reporter, commenting on Mary's unwavering commitment, had this to say: "I marvel that in such a selfish and complicated age, one woman would open herself up to the daily sufferings of so many and worry so little about herself." In the words of Mary, "We come into this world with nothing, and we leave with nothing. It's the good that we do while we're here that counts."

The good that we do for one another pays heed to the relationships that are the very fabric of reality. We are woven together with Christ and one another as a seamless garment, or as St. John Chrysostom reminds, "We are joined to one another and to Christ like flour in a loaf." As ministers, we must first be aware that we are not isolated persons or communities, but living members of a single body. Our parish is linked to the neighboring parish and to the world church. If we grasp that reality, our Christian existence will never be too small, petty, or self-centered.

This is not to say that acknowledging the truth of our connectedness makes our relationships easy. We need people who will go the extra mile to link and to heal hearts. As Jesus says, "When someone strikes you on (your) right cheek, turn the other one to him as well. If anyone wants to go to law with you over your tunic, hand him your cloak as well. Should anyone press you into service for one mile, go with him for two miles" (Mt 5:39–41). The giving of our cloak will at times signify our willingness to overlook the faults and failures of another. Rather than exposing people's foibles and shortcomings, we are challenged to clothe the naked as Jesus did; to cover them over and shelter them with the cloak of mercy while still calling them to their best selves. By God's gracious giving, we Christians are commissioned to be channels of grace and mercy to one another.

We are asked to extend God's grace not only spiritually, but also materially. Jesus continues the previous passage by saying, "Give to the one who asks of you, and do not turn your back on one who wants to borrow" (Mt 5:42). St. Peter Claver echoes Jesus' words, urging, "We must preach to the poor with our hands before we preach with our lips." We must give our cloak, our outer protections, so that others may have life. This challenges us to incredible generosity.

I was raised to understand generosity as a natural disposition of the human heart. As a child I remember many a bleak, wet winter's night on our farm in Ireland. It was not uncommon for a transient to arrive at our door, begging shelter for the night. My father's quick and ready response was always to invite the guest into our home and its heat. Food and conversation were always shared, and then my father would show our surprise visitor to a room and a bed. There were never any questions or hesitations on the part of my father. It was his natural response. In the morning, he would invite our guest to the family table for a hot breakfast, and then our guest would be on his way.

This natural disposition to generosity is not to be taken for granted. Sometimes life's experiences teach us to be more careful than carefree and generous. Perhaps we are afraid of being taken for granted. Perhaps we learn to fear because we have been taken advantage of. Perhaps we grow to be afraid that we won't have enough for ourselves.

It is so easy to give out of our abundance, to give what is left over. But it takes great faith to give out of our poverty; to experience the pinch and yet believe there will be enough for all. This is the kind of giving that makes us vulnerable, yet in releasing our material security wrapped fast around us, we become free to forge bonds of love and solidarity. Our sacrifice becomes a tangible expression of God's love in the world and our trust in that love.

This is not an easy task, but we place our confidence in a God who beckons us to laugh at the power of darkness. We will encounter disappointments in our efforts to serve, but we must not be soured by them. Attend to the words of Proverbs: "She is clothed with strength and dignity, and she laughs at the days to come" (Prv 31:25). Likewise, aware of God's blessings, the psalmist cries out, "The hills are robed with joy" (Ps 65:13). Following, we rejoice even in the midst of the darkness because we are held in a mantle of love. Etty Hillesum, the young woman and writer whose life was cut short in the Holocaust, reminds us of this love. When on the way to the gas chamber, she was asked, "How do you feel being in the clutches of the Nazis?" She responded, "I am not in the clutches of anyone but in the clutches of God and if I am in the clutches of God, then I have nothing to fear." From the train bound for Auschwitz, she threw a postcard on which she had written, "We left the camp singing."

Such was the trust of Mary McAnena who said with conviction, "God never lets me down, he is the head of my kitchen." The confident testimonies of Mary and Etty can be ours as well. We must, as Matthew's gospel proclaims, "Learn from the way the wild flowers grow. They do not work or spin. But I tell you that not even Solomon in all his splendor was clothed like one of them" (Mt 6:29).

Love wrapped in swaddling clothes, given freely and without counting the cost, is ultimately wrapped in clean linen and laid to rest in the earth. But Love rises to break the bonds of death forever and, in dazzling clothes, to declare triumph over death and destruction. Love asks us to proclaim this healing power; to summon our brothers and sisters and share the good news that, "If only I can touch his cloak, I shall be cured" (Mt 9:21). What faith to believe that God's gentle touch, God's garment of love, revives and transforms! Wrapped in this mantle of love, we go forth with renewed energy and the strength of God's power to spread our cloaks on the road, to make way for Jesus, to welcome others—the strangers—into our families, parishes, and places of work.

Finally, we pray for our world, for all its peoples, and for ourselves. We pray for the courage to believe and act with love and forgiveness. We pray that all those who have experienced the destruction of their world will not give way to despair, but will stand up tall and strong, and begin again to build a world of peace and justice. In the words of the poet Brendan Kennelly:

> Though we live in a world that dreams
>   of ending,
> that always seems about to give in,

something that will not acknowledge
    conclusion
insists that we forever begin.

Let us pray that, urged on by the love of Christ, our response
will be to "begin again" to join Jesus on the way: the way of love, the
way of forgiveness, the way of total self-giving, the way of building
right relationships with God, self, others, and all of creation.

4

A GIFT
OVERFLOWING,
A WORLD
TRANSFORMED

Those who receive the overflowing grace and gift of justice
live and reign through the one man, Jesus Christ.

Romans 5:17

In a poem titled "The Ponds," Mary Oliver once wrote, "I want to believe that the imperfections are nothing, that the light is everything." The light *is* everything. The mystery of God *is* everything. The gift poured out in Christ through the power of the Spirit lives at the heart of the universe, at the heart of all relationships, and transforms them. Today, Jesus Christ, present in the church through his Spirit, continues to scatter the seed of the word even more widely in the world, not withstanding the problems, the tensions, the discord, and the difficulties all around us. This healing presence raises us up, soothes our ills, and offers hope and salvation; it transforms the world.

We who live "between the times," between Christ's first and second coming, are filled with wonder and gratitude as we experience a gift overflowing in so many incredible ways through acts of love and service. Like the disciples on the road to Emmaus who were "disturbed" and yet "rejoiced as they recognized the Lord," we are asked to consider: What disturbs us in our church and in our world? What gives us cause to rejoice?

Our world is still aching and groaning to be filled with the fullness of Christ. What are some of the groans, the aches, that disturb us? There is the sting of war, of life lost, of the felt need to get even, of the desire to confront violence with more violence. There is the ache that comes from the inability to forgive or to deal with discord in the family and on the local, national, and international levels. There is the wound of injustice, inequity, dishonesty, poverty, and the myriad "isms" that oppress and dehumanize us.

There are many challenges that beckon us to pause. Situating ourselves and our ministries in the midst of discordant and disturbing voices, we long for one good word . . . a word of God can turn our hearts and cause us to rejoice. The poet David Whyte reminds us that "one good word is bread for a thousand." Each of us is called to find the good word in the midst of suffering and to share it with others.

The prophet Isaiah raises our sights to new levels and invites us to be a restoring presence. In a passage that is read on the first Friday of Lent every year, the prophet says that God does not desire for us to lie down in sackcloth and ashes. Rather, if we are to confront the suffering in the world, we must release the oppressed and restore justice. Isaiah proclaims that what God wants is not outward displays of penitence, but rather a fast that is transformative, a fast that brings cheer:

> This, rather, is the fasting that I wish:
> releasing those bound unjustly, untying the
> thongs of the yoke; setting free the oppressed,
> breaking every yoke; sharing your bread with
> the hungry, sheltering the oppressed and the
> homeless; clothing the naked when you see
> them, and not turning your back on your
> own. Then your light shall break forth like
> the dawn, and your wound shall quickly be
> healed; your vindication shall go before you,
> and the glory of the LORD shall be your rear
> guard. (Is 58:6–8)

What does it mean for us to release, to set free, to restore? It means that we are challenged to loosen our grip on our material goods as we reach out toward the treasure God has in store for us.

To release and restore means that we must choose the side of the voiceless and the poor as we persist in our pursuit of justice. Standing as we do in a very critical time for our nation and the world, we are challenged individually and communally to build a society in which all may prosper as human beings. It is crucial that we examine our personal and political response to violence and terrorism in light of the gospel call to nonviolence. We must also take account of the fact that much of the suffering in the world is caused by our individualism, the foreign policies of the Western world, and the distressing gap between the rich and the poor that continues to widen.

If we allow ourselves to be disturbed, the desire to release and restore hews out a place in us where we can hear the groans of our world, a space where we can allow God's extravagant love to find us and to fill us, but also to call us to the work of transformation.

We need to listen to the wisdom of the ages and believe, as the song "Between the Times" says, that "those who trust the movement of the centuries can still walk along the road between the times." We can walk along this road with a song in our hearts, confident that we, too, will rejoice because the Lord is there in the grayness of the dawn, the time between darkness and light. We draw strength from the wisdom of the centuries from testimonies of people such as Anne Frank, who wrote: "In spite of everything, I still feel that people are really good at heart. I simply cannot build up my hopes on a foundation consisting of confusion, mourning, death."

With Jessica Powers we are invited to see ourselves as ambassadors of God, citizens of love, members of a little nation whose effective weapon is love:

> Having no gift of strategy or arms,
> no secret weapon and no walled defense,
> I shall become a citizen of love. . . .

Nelson Mandela suggests that there is no easy road to freedom. None of us acting alone can achieve success. We must therefore act together as a united people for reconciliation, for nation building, for the birth of a new world.

We need a spiritual anchoring, a connectedness with the community of faith to sustain us between the times. As faithful disciples, we are called to a spirituality of deep trust. We know that the same worldly pull that draws us away from God ironically creates an emptiness in our hearts. That emptiness moves us to search for God. The gift overflowing in Christ is given to us that we might know the length, breath, and depth of this lavish God. Regardless of pressures and dilemmas, we are carried along by a force greater than ourselves.

This greater force is absolute trust. Standing in the security that this trust engenders, we can take the risk to face our own demons, to fast from our fears, to discover God's transforming flame burning at the center of our being—burning fiercely enough to consume any toxin.

We "who live between the times" must remember that no half measures are adequate when we become immersed in the life of discipleship. There is no tameness to what God offers. The Spirit helps us, plunges us into God, draws us to the crucified One, and impels us to live and proclaim Christ's liberating message. We "who live between the times" must be people who sow and plant seeds of hope. We must be forever starting over with new vigor and fresh hope, as the poet Brendan Kennelly bids us to do:

> Though we live in a world that dreams
>   of ending
> That always seems about to give in,
> Something that will not acknowledge
>   conclusion
> Insists that we forever begin.

And so we begin again. Shaped and renewed by a gift poured out in love and forgiveness, formed by a releasing that moves us to compassion, we direct our gaze outward and pray: Gift overflowing, transform us, transform our world.

5

LIFT YOUR GAZE, SEE ANEW!

> I shut my eyes and all the world drops dead . . .
> I lift my eyes and all is born again.
>
> **Sylvia Plath**

Indeed all is born again as we wake up each morning to an astounding grace-filled world of color, shape, and texture that is pure gift. We watch the sun drift over the horizon and behold the night give way to day; we bow in gratitude, we welcome. With the poet, we acknowledge and give thanks for the wonders of God's works.

> i thank You God for this most amazing day . . .
> and for everything
> which is natural, which is infinite, which is yes
> —e.e. cummings

Each day we lift our gaze and see anew. We are invited to open wide not only our physical eyes, but also the eyes of our heart, the eyes of memory. And as we do we see beyond and beneath. Whole panoramas of goodness and beauty open up to us and we recognize the sacred at the heart of all reality.

But somewhere along the way, this wide-eyed openness, this sheer delight in what lies before us wanes; we no longer notice—wonder leaks out. We become shortsighted and settle for a life of routine through which we often sleepwalk. A story is told about waking up to this light within:

> The disciple says to the master, "All my life, I have searched for meaning."
>
> "The meaning is in the search," said the master, waving off the man's distress.
>
> "Then I will never find the meaning."
>
> "No," said the master, "you will never stop looking."
>
> The master held his voice for a moment, unsure if he had been too harsh.
>
> "My friend," the master began again, "know that you are a man with a lantern who goes in search of a light."

And so we are called today to wake up to the lantern within us. If only we would open our eyes to God's dream, unfolding through the incredible power of the Spirit as Jesus walks among us. If only, like the man born blind in John's gospel, we would cry out, "Rabbi, I want to see." If only we would lift our gaze to acknowledge the brokenness, the poverty, the need in the midst of the plenty.

The prophets of our tradition have something to tell us about lifting our gaze and seeing anew. They looked at the world situation —the social, political, and spiritual environment—and saw the possibility of something different. They called for a world of justice and harmony, a world that places the God of life, the true God, at the center. "Let your eyes look straight ahead and your glance be directly forward" (Prv 4:25). Standing in the now with all of its uncertainties, its disappointments, they held on to God's faithful promise in covenant. Strengthened and encouraged, they drew wisdom from the promise that prompted them to imagine new possibilities, miracles of grace.

Think about the vision recounted by the prophet Isaiah:

Streams will burst forth
Opposites will be reconciled
Light will be poured out
The sightless will see again.

Jesus, the great prophet and the Messiah, fulfilled this hope. He enfleshed the vision, gave witness to a different way—the way of God's reign. He proclaimed a welcoming and inclusive vision where everyone experiences peace, nonviolence, forgiveness, and plenteous food for all.

We celebrate God's reign—both now and not yet. We live in that not-yet time, a time when we must continually open our eyes anew and behold again and again the outrageous love of God, a God who continues to name us good and precious; who invites us to be wide-eyed, prophetic, and visionary. God gives us eyes to see with.

A story told by the journalist Anna Quindlen calls us to this wide-eyed stance:

> I found one of my best teachers at Coney Island. . . . It was December, and I was doing a story about how the homeless suffer in the winter months. He and I sat at the edge of the wooden supports, dangling our feet over the side, and he told me his schedule, pan-handling the boulevard and sleeping in a church when the temperature was below freezing. But he told me most of the time he

stayed on the boardwalk, facing the water. I
asked him why. And he stared out at the ocean
and said, "Look at the view, young lady. Look
at the view." Words of wisdom from a man
without a dime in his pocket, nowhere to go,
no place to be. "Look at the view."

Look at the view and see the reign of God in a fresh new way.
This reign of God is what is unique about our vision. It is the lens
through which we discern the shape of our lives and our ministries. We stand at this particular moment in history, living between the now and the not yet, between memory and hope. And
then we set out with "eyes on the prize," hearts centered on God's
reign, and a vision of radical transformation for all.

We may not be able to answer every need or respond to every
call. We will inevitably feel the anguish of those who experience
oppression and dehumanization in all of its facets. We may not
be able to feed all the hungry people, bind up all the wounds, or
evangelize all who long for meaning and purpose. But we can,
with God's Spirit and with the support and encouragement of one
another, live differently. In God lies the possibility for us to give
flesh and blood witness to a more gentle, gracious, and just world.
We can nurture rich inner resources that will enable us to stand
against compromised worldly values. We can model and value the
commitments we espouse, and if we do, we can then bequeath the
vision to the next generation.

It is one thing to desire a better future, but another to recognize what's lacking in the present. Only if we do that can we direct
our energies to building the kind of future that is God's dream,
the fullness of Christ's reign here on earth. As leaders, we must
honestly confront questions such as:

- What vision do we hold for our communities of faith?

- What next steps must we take to strengthen and focus our evangelizing and formational processes?
- How do we affirm lifelong formation that puts adults at the center without forgetting children and youth?
- How do we enliven our liturgies?
- How do we extend our hospitality, our stewardship, to welcome difference?

As disciples, we are called to stand amidst the cries of the world and beg, in the name of Jesus, for change and renewal. We call out until someone, somewhere, hears and responds to the cries and aches of the poor, the immigrant, the disenfranchised, the hurt.

The eyes of faith see Jesus waiting to be asked for the sight that bathes the world in the light of God. Jesus longs to fill us with wisdom so that we can truly discern and recognize God's voice among the many voices that claim our attention. St. Paul prays, "May the eyes of [your] hearts be enlightened, that you may know what is the hope that belongs to his call" (Eph 1:18). And with the psalmist we cry out, "I raise my eyes toward the mountains. From where will my help come? My help comes from the LORD, the maker of heaven and earth" (Ps 121:2–3).

It would do us well to note the advice of a Jewish sage: "Never pray in a room without a window." We must continually stretch the margins of our lives, widen our spheres, and take the risk to move out of our comfort zones to a gracious vastness. Too many of us are blind to our blessings, and some of our eyes are darkened by prejudice and fear. The distractions of a disturbing world can stifle and block our vision. Our house becomes cluttered and filled with trivia. We lose a sense of wonder, and without wonder, our energies for living will be diminished by anxiety and resentment. We close in on ourselves and become self-focused.

It is all too easy for us to hold on to images of others that are small and dingy, mean-spirited, and not grant them the possibility of change, of turning toward the light. The stereotypes that we create serve to build walls between us. We refuse to imagine that people can change, grow, and become a new creation. Anne Sexton writes, "I would like to bury the hating eyes under the sand somewhere."

It is grace that halts us on our tracks and invites us to bury these destructive images, to tear down walls so that we may see the sun rise again, to step out of our narrow confines so that we can see anew. The late poet and spiritual writer John O'Donohue speaks about that generosity of spirit that we need: "When we look into the heart, may our eyes have the kindness and reverence of candlelight."

Contemplation is a way of being open to the surprise of God who ever comes in the rustling of trees, in the cry of a baby, in the quiet or in the chaos of traffic, in our leisure, and in our prayer. Ralph Waldo Emerson reminds us that "the sky is the daily bread of our lives."

Not only do we see God in beauty, but also in the commonplace and even the ugly. The British poet Wilfred Owen, reflecting on his experience in World War I, wrote, "I saw God through mud." When we encounter difficulties, weaknesses, disappointments in ourselves and others, we wrestle with the not so beautiful. We can—perhaps to our own amazement—find God in the pain, in the weakness, and in the struggle. We are surprised by grace; and so we must acknowledge that God hides in the depth of all.

Despite being confined by the Nazis in Tegel Prison, with his hands shackled day and night, a Jesuit priest named Alfred Delp was able to affirm God's presence in the struggle. He wrote:

> The world is ever so full of God. From the pores
> of every living thing, he seemingly reaches out
> to us. Yet, we frequently turn a blind eye to
> him. We become stuck in both beautiful and
> bad moments, failing to experience them.

Everything—every event, situation, or experience—has the potential to echo a word of hope, or peace, or of challenge. We must savor our experiences, see through them, and ask, "What is there of God in this for me? How is God present in this experience?"

Etty Hillesum, a Jewish prisoner in another concentration camp, saw goodness and graciousness even in her German guards. That is the ability and willingness to see with the heart, to see as God sees. It does not justify the situation. It does not minimize or deny the difficulty or the pain, but it can and does change the texture, the fabric of the heart.

All of us live in various shades of darkness and under common shadows. "They have eyes but do not see," Ezekiel complained (Ez 12:2). Healing the blind (in all of its meanings) was a mission close to Jesus' heart. We recall not only his many miracles, but also his encounter with the disciples on the road to Emmaus when "their eyes were opened and they recognized him" (Lk 24:31).

Do we recognize Christ's presence? Or are we blind and dull to the marvelous conversation of Christ? Do we walk through life groping our way, or perhaps looking the other way? This contemporary rendering of Psalm 73 expresses it well:

> God is good
> But I nearly missed it
> Missed seeing God's presence
> I was looking the other way. . . .

Indeed, we need one another. We need the community in our journey; to guide, to help us see anew. There is the story of Jacob the Baker:

> A neighbor of Jacob's needed to start on a journey, but it was the middle of the night.
>
> Afraid to begin, afraid not to begin, he came to Jacob. "There is no light on the path," he complained.
>
> "Take someone with you," counseled Jacob.
>
> "Jacob, what do you mean? If I do that, there will be two blind people."
>
> "You are wrong," said Jacob. "If two people discover each other's blindness, it is already growing light."

Wherever we are today on our journey, let us remember that Jesus placed his hands on the eyes of the man born blind, who was then able to see clearly. And so let us seek to become like the blind beggar. Let us look in God's direction and truly lift our eyes from our own unsettling times of fear, loss, and hurt to see anew the gracious and glorious presence of the God of sight.

6

⟪❀⟫

STAND IN THE LIGHT

God said, "Let there be light," and there was light.
God saw how good the light was.

Genesis 1:3–4

In the beginning, light flooded all of creation, giving of itself freely
and filling every available space. Today, we stand in that same light.
With the psalmist we proclaim, "In your light we see light" (Ps
36:10). And with the evangelist John, we affirm, "The light shines
in the darkness, and the darkness has not overcome it" (Jn 1:5). Like
the three companions in the moment of his transfiguration, we are
drawn into a profound experience, a memory of Jesus in dazzling
light, revealing the presence, the glory, the face of God. A memory,
yes, but also an enduring reality, a light that never fades and indeed
never burns out. A light that the darkness cannot overpower.

Each day, we stand afresh in God's light—a lamp for our feet
and a light for our eyes. As the poet Elizabeth Barrett Browning
exclaimed,

> Earth's crammed with heaven,
> and every common bush afire with God;
> But only he who sees, takes off his shoes . . .

God, who is "robed in light as with a cloak" (Ps 104:2), pours light into us, illuminates our whole beings. And we come to know our own glory.

Listen to these words by the fourteenth-century Muslim poet Hafiz:

> One day the sun admitted,
> I am just a shadow.
> I wish I could show you
> The Infinite incandescence
> That has cast my brilliant image!
> I wish I could show you,
> When you are lonely or in darkness,
> The astonishing Light
> Of your own Being.

Do we acknowledge the "astonishing light of our own being," our own goodness? Do we affirm with the psalmist that "every face turned toward him grows brighter" (Ps 34:6) and is never ashamed?

If we will stand in the light, it will show us the way, brighten our paths. But the light also casts shadows. And so, standing in the light also summons us to attend to the shadow side of our lives. Patricia Livingston recounts a story about her grandson, George, who, at age four, was so excited about going to preschool that he jumped out of bed and headed straight for the bathroom. But he missed the doorway and ran smack into the wall. His grandmother, who heard the crash, called out, "George, George, are you alright?" "I'm okay," he replied slowly, "It's just I guess I have too much dark in my eyes."

Like little George, all of us can carry too much dark in our eyes. It is a darkness that can envelop us when we give way to negativity . . . when by a word, a look, or a comment, we tear down rather than build up. We have too much dark in our eyes when we are wrapped up in our own agendas, obsessed by status, let our inner compulsions have their way, or are weighed down by worry and fear and unable to move on with life. Like the poet Rabindranath Tagore, we may wonder:

> Why did the lamp go out . . .
> I smothered it with my coat,
> to protect it from the storm
> that's why the lamp went out.

We wonder: What do we smother, refuse to cherish, and not let flourish? What fences do we construct to protect our own comfort zones?

We don't have to let the lamp go out. The greatness that we carry is ours if we choose to let it shine. If we choose largeness of heart, openness to difference, if we choose to let God's light save us from the limitations of self, it will shine. Let us choose to stand in the light.

Often, the struggles of life can focus the light. They are a gift in disguise. The poet Mary Oliver reminds us of this when she writes, "Someone I love gave me a box of darkness. It took me years to understand that that too was a gift." In the inevitable difficulties of our journey, light often soaks in through the cracks. In unexpected upheaval, we encounter God in new places and in new experiences. We recall that in every challenge there is the potential for growth, in every struggle there is an opportunity to carve out new directions. Strangely enough, the moment of weakness or brokenness is often the time when the real message of transformation can take place.

In the novel *The Life of Pi*, a young boy trying to survive in a small boat is adrift in the sea. With him is a wild tiger, who he names Richard Parker. He describes his desolation and his attempts to fight the darkness away. Through ritual, through thoughts of his family, and finally through the struggle, light burst forth. He writes, "The blackness would stir and eventually go away, and God would remain, a shining point of light in the dark. I would go on loving." Reflecting on such experiences, we are led to ask, in the words of Sue Monk Kidd, "And does God not meet each of us, hold us as we too brave the swirling darkness and the confusion, as we too wrestle with the daily struggles in search of peace, in search of answers, and in search of wholeness?"

Light has the power to brighten the dark and dingy corners of our life, the places that we often want to hide from, cover up, deny, and pretend not to see. Ralph Waldo Emerson says:

> Indeed, Light is the first of painters.
> There is no object so frail
> That intense light will not
> Make it beautiful.

We are called to summon up the courage "to climb out of our narrow confines onto a ledge of light," as suggested by Jessica Powers. In other words, we are called to let go of anxiety and the need to control, and to discern those movements that come from the Spirit of Light from those that come from the spirit of darkness. Then we can utter a wholehearted yes to the invitations that are of God and keep our lamp burning even when the wick burns low.

On a light-filled path we can stride with confidence, for the way is clear. But what do we do when we approach a darkened stretch? Do we panic and turn back, or do we ask for the courage to face the obstacles, confident that the light will penetrate the darkness? At times like these, we can take small steps forward when we reach out in care for another, or when we offer a word of hope or encouragement. At times like these, we need the support of family and friends who continue to believe in us, who are there to assure us that all will be well in spite of our hesitancy to believe in the light. At times like these, we need to withdraw to the quiet, cling to the lamp of wisdom within, and remember silence can nourish and repair the soul. Indeed, when God gifts us with an experience of his loving presence, then we realize that all our troubles are transitory.

Being full of light, we become a source of light and a witness for others. The most gracious and courageous gift that we can give the world is the gift of our true selves. We let our lives speak, and letting our lives speak challenges us to authenticity, to transparency. A wise saying calls us to the simplicity of light-bearing when it says, "It only takes a single lamp to bring light to a valley that has been dark for a thousand years."

I am reminded here of Immaculée Ilibagiza, who shared her miraculous story of survival during the Rwandan genocide in 1994. She and seven other women were forced to hide and to huddle silently together in a cramped bathroom two feet by four feet. She described her horrendous experience of helplessness and of vulnerability, and yet her deep trust that God was near. Her faith in God sustained her. It was, as the Indian poet Rabindranath Tagore wrote, "a faith that feels the light and sings when the dawn is dark." Immaculée wrote,

> I literally felt the fear pumping through my veins, and my blood was on fire. I struggled to form an image of God in my mind, envisioning two pillars of brilliant white light burning in front of me, like two giant legs. I wrapped my arms around the legs, like a frightened child clinging to His mother. I begged God to fill me with His light and strength, to cast out the dark energy from my heart. I'm holding onto you, God, and I do not doubt but you can save me. I will not let go of you until you send the killers away.

Immaculée stood in the light, believed in the light, clung to the promise, and became a source of light and hope for her six companions.

What about us? We, too, are summoned to share the light of faith, to bring others not only in touch with, but in communion and intimacy with, Jesus. It is Jesus who laid out a vision for a new humanity, who disturbed, who shared enduring values. There are many ways of spreading light, but two in particular come to mind: to be a candle that radiates light and to be a mirror that reflects light.

There is a painful price in being the candle. For just as a candle consumes itself as it radiates brightness, so, too, must we be willing to pour out our lives in love and compassion as Jesus did. Viktor Frankl, Holocaust survivor, suggests, "What is to give light, must endure burning." We die in order to be born. We recall that the hope and light of the world burst forth from the cross, and that we cannot run away from it.

Being a mirror of God's light challenges us to take responsibility for nurturing our communities of faith. St. John Chrysostom reminds us that when we live from a core of love, from an attitude that puts others before self, we will mirror light, a light that will overflow into the everyday, into the ordinary. For example: When we make space in our daily schedule to listen to another . . . we are light. When everyone else is ready to give up on a teenager and we choose to speak on his/her behalf . . . we are light. When we get outside of ourselves and visit the lonely or the housebound, or welcome the stranger . . . we are light. When we live out of a sense of gratitude and joy in uneasy times . . . we are light.

The final word of history does not belong to war, discord, or gloom, but to peace, harmony, and radiance. William Blake could see past the ordinary world and glimpsed the light of the beyond:

To see a world in a grain of sand
And a heaven in a wild flower.
Hold infinity in the palm of your hand
And eternity in an hour.

In other words, to look for the sparkle in the ordinary, the mystery in the everyday.

Where is the light leading us? Are we ready to take a step into the unfamiliar, the unknown? Are we ready to share our light? All of us are called to be visionaries in one way or another. Each of us holds part of the truth. Together, we give shape to the future. We must trust the future. The poet Patrick Overton puts it well:

When we walk to the edge of all the light that we have and take step into the darkness of the unknown, we must believe that one of two things will happen. There will be something solid for us to stand on or we will be taught to fly.

We are here to be light, to bring out God's hue, God's color, in the world. Imagine the transformation if we made a commitment to flood our world with God's brightness, with positive energy, with forgiveness and compassion. What if together we spread light over our families, over those who struggle, our communities, over warring nations, or our planet?

The "what ifs" are many, but the call is one: to stand in the light and continue to spill out the amazing light of our own being, the astounding light of God at the center of all that we can hope to be for our world.

7

STEP INTO FREEDOM

Lazarus, come out!

John 11:43

Like Lazarus, we are called to come out of our tombs, to come forth to a life that is brand new. Jesus poured light into that darkened corner where Lazarus thought he might rest secure forever. This same Jesus invites us today to open up the corners of our hearts to his liberating presence, to his gift of light. He calls us to embrace a brand-new, spacious life, not only for ourselves, but for all humankind.

Jesus, the life-giver, raises hope and invites us to an appreciation of the utter wide-openness and graciousness of God. He urges us to abandon all that belittles us and stand fast by the liberty that he gives us. St. Paul reminds us, "Where the Spirit of the Lord is, there is freedom" (2 Cor 3:17).

Learning to let go of our fears and anxieties is the first step. As we do this, we begin to see more clearly; we gain positive energy to deal with our demanding reality. To let go is to choose to bid farewell to our dingy tomblike existence and to everything that constrains us, to stretch toward the light. Some people won't dare take the risk. They become so accustomed to the tomb that they find solace in it. It is not so much that they like it, but they are unable to imagine a different place. They would prefer to be unhappy in their familiar situation rather than risk the unfamiliar, and so they remain trapped.

Megan McKenna tells the story of a young man who decided to clean out his fish tank. The first problem was where to put the fish while he did the cleaning. He decided on the bathtub. He transported the fish, dumped them into their luxurious temporary quarters, and went to work cleaning the tank. It took hours, but finally there was fresh water, new algae, and stones along the bottom. When he went back to the bathtub for the fish, he was startled to find what they were doing in their large tub.

They were not swimming its length and breadth. In fact, they were occupying the exact amount of space they had left behind in the tank. He was fascinated. He tried to get them to move out of their self-imposed prison. He ruffled the water. No response. He poured their food way down at the opposite end. No response. He created waves with the water. They stayed put.

He finally gave up, took them back and dumped them into the clean tank, and began to wonder: Do I live like those fish? Do I limit myself by past experiences and knowledge, content to stay safe where I am? Have I been moved up to a huge bathtub, but I still swim around like I'm in a small tank?

We might ask ourselves the same questions.

There are times when we feel bound up like Lazarus. The winding, twisting roads of life have their way of limiting our vision. We are plunged into experiences of grayness, of insecurity, of drabness and dinginess of spirit—unable to function.

Freedom, as Mahatma Gandhi once said, "is never dear at any price. It is the breadth of life." It is a gift unbounded, graciously poured out, and yet so often we allow ourselves to become crippled, imprisoned. We forget to trust in Christ, the resurrection and the life, who awakens fresh stirrings of divine life in us.

The poet David Whyte reminds us that "anything or anyone that does not bring you alive is too small for you." What is too small for us? What keeps us from the fullness of who we are called to be, and from blossoming into the gift God intends us to become? Fears both real and imaginary, inner snarls, and discord turn us in on ourselves, blind us to the goodness within our brokenness and to the beauty of all of creation.

We also relinquish our freedom when we cling to personal power, seek recognition, and are frightened of losing our good name. We become slaves to our own needs; we deny our very humanity; we forget who and whose we really are. Our hearts become two sizes too small. Setting out on this road to freedom is rarely easy; it involves a real struggle. To choose freedom is to know who we are, with all that is beautiful, authentic, and with all that is raveled and tattered in us.

It is to acknowledge, in the words of Gandhi, "My imperfections and failures are as much a blessing from God as my successes and talents and I lay them both at his feet." It is to cherish values that fortify, to embrace them and cultivate them; it is to be anchored in a vision of wholeness and truth, open to newness and hope for a brighter future. This freedom that we seek is more than a release from our tombs or an escape from slavery. As Nelson Mandela once said, freedom is "not merely to cast off one's chains, but to live in a way that respects and enhances the freedom of others."

Our risen Christ wants desperately to reach into our dark and worn places, to invite, to entice, and if need be, to pry us free. In the end, it is not our own strength or courage that will get us over these fearful cliffs that seem impossible to climb. Grace alone will lead us to the other side.

During the Nazi occupation of Holland, Corrie ten Boom and her father hid many Jews in their home. The story is told of how they found the courage to do this when they began to recognize the trouble that was coming with the Nazi invasion.

Corrie said to her father, "How will we ever face up to what's coming?" Her father said, "Corrie, when you were a little girl and you used to go on the train to Amsterdam—when did I give you your ticket for the train?" Corrie said, "You always put the ticket in my hand just when I was getting on the train." "That's right, Corrie," her father said, "and it will be the same now. God will give us our ticket, the grace and the freedom when we need it."

History is filled with stories of women and men who refused to be stifled, refused to surrender the hope that beauty could be restored in the midst of ruin, refused to get caught up in power and privilege, people who have hung in there, stayed the course, people such as Rosa Parks, who declared, "The only tired I was, was tired of giving in," and she chose not to give in. She uttered her "no."

Think about those around us who have fled from oppressive economic situations—refugees, immigrants, victims of human trafficking. Freedom was taken from them. They live in our midst, yet often through fear of being rejected or misunderstood they have to hide their identity and pretend to be someone else. They live encased in fear and insecurity, and are forced to discover delicate ways of evasion to protect themselves from further hurt.

To be free is to discover new insights in the stuff of life. It is to accept limitations in ourselves and others. It is to know that when we belong to a community, a parish, a household, or a nation, that none of these is perfect, that each has its mixture of light and dark. Indeed, our fears and weaknesses are often a gift in disguise; they hew out a place in us where we can experience the extravagant love of God present not only in our alleluia moments but in our times of struggle as well.

According to Robert Frost, "Freedom lies in being bold." Ultimately, our freedom is for love and compassion, signaling us to participate in the advent of freedom for all. It is to reach out and help lift burdens, unwrap bindings so that others may come to experience the expansiveness of God's freeing presence. Trust in God raises us up to begin again, doing our part to make the world a smiling and positive place.

And so we ask:

- Can we reasonably dream for a world where people— whatever race, religion, culture, or economic situation, whatever the age or gender—can find a place and reveal their gifts?
- Can we imagine a world community of peace, and refuse to be so dreadfully torn by the ravishes of war?
- Can we hope for a society, a church, where each of us is a critical and essential part in the harmony and function of the whole?
- Can we imagine a world, a community of integrity, where millions of women and children are no longer trafficked, sold, or exploited as sex objects?
- Can we commit to welcoming, inviting, including the stranger, the immigrant, the one in need?
- Can we realistically embrace the responsibility inherent in our leadership roles and boldly spell out the contours of the reign of God among us here and now, together with the promise of liberty, of holiness, and truth?

- Can we muster up the courage to let go of all that dampens our spirits and live even joyously with our own struggles?

The road to attaining and bringing freedom is a long and grueling one, as recounted by Nelson Mandela:

> I have walked the long road to freedom. I have tried not to falter; I have made missteps along the way. But I have discovered the secret that after climbing a great hill, one only finds that there are many more hills to climb. I have taken a moment here to rest, to steal a view of the glorious vista that surrounds me, to look back on the distance I have come. But I can rest only for a moment, for with freedom comes responsibilities, and I dare not linger; for my long walk is not yet ended.

We, too, dare not linger, for our long walk is not yet ended; for some it has only begun. We are summoned again and again to rise from the tomb of indifference and fear, and step into a life of freedom, however demanding that letting go might be.

Freedom does not only come when the anguish is over. It can also be experienced in the struggle. Like Lazarus's sisters, Martha and Mary, we wonder, "Where were you? Did you forget? Did you not hear?" And then in the midst of the murkiness comes the insight. God is right there in the struggle gracing us with strength, leading us to find meaning in the pain, and digging out greater wisdom in us. In the pain, we discover a God who invites us into a love that set fire to a bush in the desert, forced open graves, and enabled the dead to walk again.

Resurrection means getting up again, finding hope again no matter what challenges we face. Confident that God walks with us and holds us up as we journey, we embrace fresh hope, a largeness of heart, and remember the call to step into freedom is not only for us, but also for the transformation and restoration of the whole world.

8

⟪☙⟫

EMBRACE AND ECHO THE WORD

Indeed, the word of God is living and active,
sharper than any two-edged sword. . . .

Hebrews 4:12

We are called to embrace the word and allow it to resound in ourselves, our homes, our communities, and indeed, throughout the
world. The word of God that we embrace is alive and active. It is
a word that drops down from heaven and transforms the earth, a
word that does not return empty. It is the word that became flesh
and walked this earth. It made visible the invisible, healed and
loved and transformed, a word that continues to be active right
here, right now.

St. Amadeus wrote in the twelfth century:

> Lord, we have heard your word, and we have
> been astounded. We have pondered your
> marvels and we have fainted. As your word
> descended, our hearts have been melted. You

> shed light in the darkness, dew upon dryness,
> and in the bitter frost, you kindled a raging
> fire.

Do we allow God to shed light in our darkness, dew upon our dryness, and kindle in us a raging fire? Are we astounded by the word of God? Do we embrace the word and allow it to change our hearts, our ways of relating and loving, our ways of teaching and preaching?

Remember the story of the call of Samuel. God called him as a boy while he was ministering in the temple. The first two times Samuel heard the voice, he mistook it for Eli's. Then,

> The Lord called Samuel again, a third time. And he got up and went to Eli, and said, "Here I am, for you called me." Then Eli perceived that the Lord was calling the boy. Therefore Eli said to Samuel, "Go, lie down; and if he calls you, you shall say, 'Speak, Lord, for your servant is listening.'" So Samuel went and lay down in his place. Now the Lord came and stood there, calling as before, "Samuel! Samuel!" And Samuel said, "Speak, for your servant is listening."

God called out to Samuel and Samuel was there, with an open heart, a readiness to hear. Are we ready when God calls? Are we collected at our center, or are we off center? Do the words just skim the surface, or do we really listen to the voice of God?

What holds us back from listening with the heart? Perhaps our hearts have grown dull and cold, hardened by life's struggles, no longer absorbent, spongelike. Maybe our hearts are twisted or entangled and have lost the sense of truth about ourselves, about others, and about God. Perhaps we have bruised hearts that are so self-focused that we don't have the ability to trust and allow fresh new life to be breathed upon us. Maybe our hearts are a few sizes too small.

The great poet Jessica Powers wrote in "This Is a Beautiful Time":

> Oh, hear Him within you speaking this
> infinite love. . .
> lifting the sky of the soul with the expansions
> of light,
> shaping new heights and new depths. . . .

If we are to hear God speaking this infinite love and lifting our souls to new heights, we must do what the prophet Ezekiel did: "Son of man . . . feed your belly and fill your stomach with this scroll I am giving you. I ate it, and it was as sweet as honey in my mouth" (Ez 3:3). What does it mean for us to eat the scroll, the word? It means that if our teaching is to have wisdom and power, it must flow from a spirituality that is Christ-centered, holistic, and committed to the agenda of the gospel. We must echo good news to a world in need of direction, meaning, and beauty, a world in need of a morality that respects all of life and of a love that enfolds and holds all creation.

Once upon a time, a student asked her master, "What is the difference between one who has wisdom and knowledge and someone who is enlightened?" The teacher responded immediately, "Easy. The one who has wisdom and knowledge is the one who carries a candle in the darkness and lights the way. The one who is enlightened has become the torch itself."

And so we are invited to eat the word, a word that is sweet as honey even when it is challenging, painful, and risky. It is in the savoring that the word becomes sweet. St. Anselm calls us to savor the word:

> Come now, turn aside for a while from your
> daily employment. Escape for a moment

from the tumult of your thoughts. Put aside
your weighty cares, let your burdensome
distractions wait. Free yourself awhile for God
and rest awhile in him.

Not only do we embrace the word, but we are embraced by
the word, caught up in God's life. "The soul is in God, and God is
in the soul," said St. Catherine of Siena. Being caught up in God's
life is what sends us forth to proclaim the word to a world looking for life. Jesus is not dead; he is alive, and so we can proclaim
resurrected hope.

If we are to be bearers, interpreters, and echoers of God's
word, then we must be persons of vision: women and men who
believe in the creative and renewing power of the Spirit. We must
be freed from the need to prove ourselves, the need to hold on to
the security of the tried and true, and to resist stepping into the
unknown. Leadership calls us to be risk-takers and choose a mission over maintenance approach to ministry. A mission approach
keeps us enthusiastic and sends us out with an urgency, a passion
to be at the service of the reign of God. A maintenance approach
keeps us drawing out the same old tedious, lifeless approaches and
models to sharing good news that do not inspire or move hearts.
Rather, we must be people who explore new territory. We must
believe that the seeds of the new millennium are forgiveness, liberation, and holiness. What new seeds, new models, new visions
are we nourishing for the generation that is with us and the generation to follow us?

Our ministry is often demanding and at times unappreci-
ated, and we must be willing to accept the stresses that abound
around us, trust in a provident God and live like human beings in
a world where the full force of Christ's resurrection and the work
of the Spirit have not yet been felt. We can do this if we embrace

the word, eat the word, and believe that God is with us in the struggles, as the early Christians did.

To echo the word, we must be willing to know and share our real selves, our weaknesses as well as our strengths. Discovering and believing in one's self is a major human task in a world disoriented by sin. Bishop Howard Hubbard stated:

> Remember, your ministry as a catechist arises from the need of the community, and what the community most needs today in those who minister is not a walking theology manual, but sensitive and caring human beings who are willing to share their humanity with others by being there in the thick of things, in the midst of their struggles, and by paying loving attention to them.

We are called to be jubilant, carefree ministers who can laugh at the power of darkness. Children laugh at least five hundred times a day; adults maybe three times. St. Ephraim wrote, "I will give praise during my lifetime, I will not be a dead person among the living." Our presence, body language, and words must radiate the message that we are delighted to be here, delighted to be bearers of good news. That is why it is important to step back to gain the balance and perspective.

St. Niceta, a fourth-century bishop, shares some wisdom in this regard:

> When it is too dark for you to see, seek Christ, for he is the light. Are you sick? Have recourse to him who is both doctor and health. Are you afraid of this or that? Remember that on all occasions, he will stand by your side like an angel.

As Christ stands with us, so we stand with him. And to stand by his side is to be a person of prayer. Prayer makes us disappear into God. We believe that there is a God-shaped hole in all of us that only God can fill. This is God's dwelling place within us. Our vocation is to speak from the place in us where God dwells.

What we cherish in our hearts and declare with our mouth, we must attempt to fulfill in our deeds. And so we are called to proclaim not only the comforting words of the gospel, but the gospel's challenge as well. As Walter Burghardt points out:

> We must recognize that a wound in one is a hurt in each, that as long as one child falls asleep hungry at night, my stomach hurts; that as long as an elderly person can't afford heat, or fears tomorrow, there is a chill in my bones; or that as long as one person is treated with a lack of dignity, I am ashamed. Indeed, we must affirm a profound biblical truth that the face of the poor is the face of God.

Let us ask God to shed light upon our darkness and dew upon our dryness. Let us pray that the Spirit will kindle in us a hunger for the word and allow it to resound in our lives, our families, our communities, our places of work; and, indeed, throughout the world.

9

STEEPED IN MERCY, BALM FOR THE WORLD

By the tender mercy of our God,
The dawn from on high will break upon us.

Luke 1:78

We have been steeped over and over again in God's extravagant, tender mercy—freely offered, freely given. It is a balm for our souls, balm for the world. The poet Denise Levertov reminds us:

> As swimmers dare
> To lie face to the sky
> And water bears them,
> As hawks rest upon air
> And air sustains them,
> So would I learn to attain
> Freefall and float
> Into Creator Spirit's deep embrace,

Knowing no effort earns
That all surrounding grace.

That mercy . . . grace . . . a being bathed in the compassionate love of God. The theme of God's mercy weaves through our faith tradition, and God never tires of drawing us into this gift of all-surrounding grace poured out, overflowing. It is perhaps the most awesome of all God's qualities.

Our God "delights in clemency" (Mi 7:18). His tender compassion is renewed each day, like the rising of the sun. His mercy reaches into the dark spaces of our floundering and our faltering, our waning and our weakening. It enters there and picks us up, holds us, and surrounds us with love until we are healed.

There is not a creature that lives but savors the mercy of God. "Every bird," says Ambrose, "in its kind sings hymns of praise to God for his bounty, but men and women taste it in a more particular manner, taste the cream and quintessence of God's mercies."

And Shakespeare writes, "The quality of mercy is not strained. It dropeth as the gentle rain from heaven upon the place beneath." It is an attribute to God himself.

Yet mercy is not weak or sentimental. Scripture opens up for us some challenging experiences of God's mercy. There is Jacob, who has a mysterious encounter by the Jabbok River. Something out of the darkness assaults him and wrestles with him all night, leaving him at daybreak with his hip out of joint. Yet he is grateful to have seen God face to face and still be alive (Gn 32:31). But the question remains: What kind of God is that who wrestles with us?

Is this a God of grace and mercy, who allows us to bump into one contradiction after another, to experience the shattering of our well-laid plans, the tearing apart of our complacency? But how else might a God who loves us so ardently and passionately behave?

A God who truly cares will do everything to help us trust that even though we struggle and grapple through the ups and downs of life, like Jacob, we will finally emerge stronger, more focused, and vital. In the encounter with pain we are purified, emptied, and renewed. We die only to rise more hope-filled and grateful for the hand that has shaped us anew.

It is this tremendously caring God whom John Donne in one of his sonnets courageously implores:

> Batter my heart, three-personed God . . .
> Overthrow me, and bend
> Your force to break, blow, burn, and make
> me new . . . For I,
> Except you enthrall me, shall never be free,
> Nor chaste, except you ravish me.

This three-personed God is swift to understand and welcome back while honestly inviting us to be our best self.

If we take our human experience seriously, we will find traces of this challenging mercy and the very wisdom of God's Spirit in the joys and sorrows, hurts and triumphs of our lives. This prayer, found by the side of a dead child at a concentration camp at the end of World War II, is a supreme example of grace-filled mercy:

> O Lord,
> Remember not only the men
> And women of goodwill.
> But all those of ill will.
> But do not remember all the sufferings
> They have inflicted on us;
> Remember the fruits we have bought
> Thanks to this suffering—
> Our comradeship, our loyalty, our humility,
> Our courage, our generosity, and greatness of
> heart,

> Which has grown out of all of this,
> And when they come to judgment,
> let all the fruits which we have borne
> Be their forgiveness. Amen.

Yet another example of mercy during war is Betsie ten Boom, who steadfastly refused to hate the guards who beat her. Eventually, they beat her to death. Her dying words are both simple and profound: "We must tell the people what we have heard here. We must tell them that there is no pit so deep that he is not deeper still." Here we encounter again a God of mercy working through our struggles, showing us our goodness, as he lovingly transforms us anew. It is the journey toward freedom.

In our efforts to be merciful, we must first remember to be merciful to ourselves. Each of us feels somehow stifled, restrained, unfree. But by what? By anxiety, by a sense that we can never measure up to others' expectations. We wonder how others really judge and evaluate us, leaving us perplexed and dispirited. We hang on to our own failures and humiliations; we forget to forgive ourselves and so remain paralyzed.

Yet God has mercy on our fumblings, our failings, our pettiness, and our get-even mentality. God forgives our shortsightedness and lifts us up. Loving mercifully, God invites us to accept ourselves with our limitations and not allow them to claim ownership of us. Jessica Powers invites us to enter into the expanse of God's mercy:

> I rose up from the acres of self that I tended
>   with passion
> and defended with flurries of pride;
> I walked out of myself and went into the
>   woods of God's mercy,
> and here I abide. . . .

And I fear God no more; I go forward to
   wander forever
in a wilderness made of His infinite mercy
   alone.

The question is: What does belief in this God of infinite mercy invite us to be and call us to do? To begin, we must admit that we are often blind to the fact that the greed, wars, and violence that we see played out on the world stage (and for which we criticize our leaders) are, to a large extent, amplifications of what is happening inside our hearts and in our personal relationships. The larger world that sometimes seems to threaten and overwhelm us is reflective of our interior dispositions. A growing callousness in our society is often mirrored by the hardening of our own hearts. Mercy and compassion are seen as signs of weakness rather than as the powerful gospel response of the Samaritan or the call of the beatitudes. But consider a moment how different our lives might be were we to live with compassion and to show mercy. Perhaps our relationships with our parents, our children, our siblings might be renewed and made more whole, if we loosened our grip on a fear-based sense of security and instead recognized our common hurts calling out for healing. Perhaps were we to show compassion instead of judgment, we might foster an occasion of healing and wholeness rather than one of hurt or alienation.

And so we are challenged to live the Sermon on the Mount, to check up on our spiritual vision, make adjustments, and strive to see with God's eyes. It means developing a heart so large, so magnanimous, that one could not entertain the thought of worshipping God without first settling differences with one's neighbor. It is a stance that shuns judging the faults and foibles of others, and assuming a posture that is always respectful and merciful and gracious to the names of others. It is an openness to transformation as promised through the prophet Ezekiel: "I will give you a new heart and place a new spirit within you" (Ez 36:26). It is an attitude that mirrors God's compassionate and tender care for all of us, for all peoples. When we refuse to judge, we begin the process of quieting the demons of our own lives and the power that they exercise over our brothers and sisters.

St. Catherine of Genoa received a mystical insight that the gates of heaven are wide open. She says, "As far as paradise, God has placed no doors there. Whoever enters there does so. All merciful God stands with arms open waiting to receive us into glory."

We are called to be merciful to the offenses of others, to be ready to show mercy to those who injure us. St. Stephen, the first martyr, "fell to his knees and cried out in a loud voice, 'Lord, do not hold this sin against them'" (Acts 7:60). When he prayed for himself, he stood, but when he came to pray for his enemies, he knelt down. St. Bernard says this was to show his earnestness in prayer and how greatly he desired that God would forgive them. This is a rare kind of mercy.

It is crucial to remember that genuine forgiveness leads to healing of relationships, but does not ask that we deny the wrong done. Although we long for healing, we find the process arduous and the thought of forgiveness somewhat disturbing. So we are tempted to allow anger to nest in our hearts or get involved in revenge. Rather, we are invited to name the wrong and not get smothered by it. Seamus Heaney counsels us, "So hope for a great sea-change on the far side of revenge—believe that a further shore is reachable from here . . . believe in miracles, cures and healing wells." Believe in the merciful compassion of God.

It is Jesus, who once laid his hands on the needy, who now lays his hands on us and requires us to do the same to the overlooked person, the poor person who comes seeking bread and hope. Jesus shows us that God must surely be compassionate, merciful, loving on the other side of every boundary.

Our challenge is to help ourselves and others see the gift of mercy that enables us to practice the attitude of mercy. Would that we could proclaim with e. e. cummings, "Now the ears of my ears are awake and now the eyes of my eyes are opened." Let us open our eyes to the need all around us, let us recognize solidarity with any part of creation that is suffering, oppressed, handicapped or victimized, to reach out and be balm for the world. We have only to glance at the news to find so many in our world today in need of our support.

Mercy moves us, as it moved Jesus, to act with love and integrity, at whatever cost; to do whatever the situation requires of us to resist, expose, advocate, remedy. It is not a puny or sentimental love, but places loving limits and consequences that are sometimes needed. It sees things as they are, sees the cruelty and pain. It looks the brokenness right in the face, takes it all in . . . and moves us to free all of creation from what is too small. Indeed, according to Albert Einstein, "Our task must be to free ourselves from this prison by widening our circles of compassion to embrace all living creatures and the whole of nature in its beauty."

Our world desperately needs us to thump on the cords of the heart and let God's merciful love enclose, encompass, wind us around. It calls us to great generosity and largeness of spirit. "The heart generous and kind most resembles God," said Robert Burns. It is remarkably difficult to cling to the illusion that life is about you when you are focused body and soul on the needs of others. You will rarely know greater happiness than when through your word, your love, your hands . . . a smile is born on the face of someone in pain. Emily Dickinson goes so far as to say:

> If I can stop one heart from breaking,
> I shall not live in vain;
> If I can ease one life the aching,
> Or cool one pain,

Or help one fainting robin
Unto his nest again
I shall not live in vain.

This mercy draws our grasping hands and energies to purposeful service and to see in our apparently flawed creation a life embraced by a God whose name is mercy. This God does not make perfection or success a criterion for love. Rather, God nudges us to remember that we are steeped in mercy, and so we can learn to attain freefall and float into Creator Spirit's deep embrace . . . knowing that no effort earns that all-surrounding grace.

10

IMAGING LOVE, EMPOWERING LIVES

Each person is a star, their soul is bright
As anything the heavens have to show.

Brendan Kennelly

God continually touches our human life, renews and transforms us in ordinary and extraordinary ways. And although God is beyond all images, scripture offers us a continual flow of images. Second Corinthians reminds us that, "All of us, gazing with unveiled face on the glory of the Lord, are being transformed into the same image from glory to glory, as from the Lord who is the Spirit" (2 Cor 4:5–8).

We are always in the process of being shaped into God's own image. God is always revealing God's self to our souls, but like surprises and sunsets, God never does it the same way twice. Each of us in our wholeness stands in a relationship to God so unique, so intimate, that God's word declares us to be "like God." We were created in the image of God. Somehow, we are like God. We are light, we are blessing, and we are hope.

Self-image and God-image are, in fact, intimately linked. As we experience new aspects of God, something more is called forth in us, our faces are unveiled, and we are opened up to increasing experience and knowledge of God's many-faceted presence in our lives. And with the psalmist we recognize that "every face turned toward God grows brighter and brighter and is never ashamed" (Ps 34:5–6).

And yet, the Genesis narrative of our first parents and the commentaries of the early church also suggest that the original image is somehow diminished. Having been created "like God" we often find ourselves collectively and individually estranged from the creative source of our being. We fail to image God.

The stark realities of our times—the specter of violence, hypocrisy, ecological irresponsibility rampant in our world—assault our sensibilities and make us painfully aware of this truth. Even in the most well-meaning circles, we discover our limitations over and over again. Our failure to communicate, our envy and narrow-mindedness, and our conviction that we alone have it right confront us at every step. Indeed, the divine image is often unrecognizable in us.

Yet for centuries Christians have held up, reflected upon, and cleaved to the image of God with us, God living and loving among us. Jesus the Christ is the image of the unseen God, as Colossians reminds us. Indeed, we have held up this multifold hallowed image of Christ in order that we might not only worship and adore him, but also grow into his image, become participants in the reality of God-with-us.

The process of restoring our original blessing and becoming the image of God in our world is gradual. It beckons us to conversion and transformation. An African schoolgirl's prayer shows us the way: "O, thou great chief, light a candle in my heart that I may see what is therein, and sweep the rubbish from my dwelling place." We have to claim the rubbish—the evil and darkness in our lives—to allow God's healing word to soften, renew, and cleanse us. Brendan Kennelly reminds us that our weakness, evil, and darkness can be a gift if we allow it to shake us out of our complacency:

> A branch beyond my reach says
> It is well for me to feel
> The transfiguring breath of evil
> Because yesterday
> The roots by which I live
> Lodged in apathetic clay
> But for that fury
> How should I be rid of the slow death?
> How should I know?
> That what a storm can do
> Is to terrify my roots and make me new

Indeed the storms and struggles of our lives can often be the means by which we face ourselves and learn to let go of the things that mar God's image in us. Standing in the presence of a transforming God, we are changed for life. And out of this transforming experience, we can empower others to go forth and face the challenge of standing in the presence of God so that they, too, can mirror God, mirror love. Thus, we together can become signs of hope, signs of the Spirit and of the Spirit's activity.

Often, we surrender our power to the anxiety we bear, to the fear, dread, and despair that eats at us. Yet hope calls us to cherish a desire with expectation of fulfillment even in the midst of doubt, ambiguity, and uncertainty. It is not a naïve expectation that all will go smoothly, that desolation and disappointment will remain a stranger. Rather, it is a conviction that God will always be with us and we can live at ease no matter what happens.

There is an Ethiopian legend about a shepherd boy named Aleymayu. It speaks to us of the power of hope. Aleymayu had to spend the night on a bitterly cold mountain. He had only a very thin cloth to cover himself. To the amazement of all the villagers, he returned alive and well. When they asked him how he survived, he replied, "The night was bitter. When all the sky was dark, I thought I would die. Then far, far off, I saw a shepherd's fire on another mountain. I kept my eyes on the red glow in the distance and I dreamt of being warm. And that is how I had the strength to survive."

Hope is openness to the future. It has to do with believing beyond today and waking up each morning knowing that our lives have a value no matter what the circumstances. Emily Dickinson wrote:

> Hope is the thing with feathers
> That perches in my soul
> And sings the tune without the words,
> And never stops at all.

When we educate, we are helping people to believe that life has meaning, that it is worth living, and that their life can make a difference on this planet. We are drawing out the hope and belief that the world can be made a better, more humane place. Yes, catechesis is empowering. It is about planting roots and giving wings—planting roots by instilling enduring values and creating milieus where hope can be awakened, nourished, and challenged; giving wings by birthing new dreams, and creating new vistas.

The early-twentieth-century poet Guillaume Apollinaire challenges us to take a risk. He writes:

Come to the edge
It's too high
Come to the edge
We might fall
Come to the edge
And they came
And she pushed them
And they flew.

This freeing, life-giving push empowers others to fly—to embrace a gospel vision of life, to imagine new possibilities, to believe in God, to believe in their power to enable newness.

Wherever we turn we find a world of contradictions between plenty and destitution: a world where most of us take a gracious home for granted while millions upon millions of refugees water the roads of exile with their tears; a world of plentiful bounty and rich harvests, but where millions are chronically undernourished; a world where thousands of our college students make it big each year while thousands of runaway kids are bought and sold in prostitution or experience the pain of hopelessness as they roam our city streets; a world of great generosity, yet a world of avarice where millions make a god of money, power, and prestige. This is the world in which we are called to image God's love, to bring hope, and to empower lives.

Wherever we turn, we hear the cries of the poor, the battered, and the bruised: the cry of those who live below the poverty line and the hundreds of thousands more for whom life is a burden, the cry of children sexually abused, the cry of adults dulled by drugs to despair or aflame with anger, the cry of the aging heartsick with loneliness. This is the world in which we are called to image God's love, to bring hope, and to empower lives.

We live in a world of paradox, a world in need of healing and empowerment. And in the midst of that paradox we "hold fast to the hope that lies before us. This we have as an anchor of the soul, sure and firm" (Heb 6:18–19). Hope is, indeed, the sure and steadfast anchor of the soul, and with that hope we can image God's love and empower others' lives.

《◎》

11

PASSION
FOR JUSTICE

Unless the eye catch fire, the God will not be seen.
Unless the ear catch fire, the God will not be heard.
Unless the heart catch fire, the God will not be loved.
Unless the mind catch fire, the God will not be known.

William Blake

A passion for justice is the fire that can change heart and mind, sight and hearing. Justice is a challenging, sobering theme, but only by way of justice do we enter into right relationship with God. The invitations to this restoration are everywhere: to seek justice, to be justice, to reach out in compassion, to care for the stranger and the one in need.

The Museum of Tolerance in West Los Angeles is one place that powerfully extends this invitation. Along its corridors, sight and sound, image and testimony, together reveal the pain of millions of people who suffered injustice, prejudice, concentration camps, the gas chamber, and Auschwitz. A very moving, overwhelming, and confrontational experience, the exhibits also express the reality of those today who endure the more subtle intolerance suffered in bigotry, racism, labeling, and riots. One caption reads: "Words break more than bones." How great is the power of words to heal or to destroy!

You begin the museum journey in the "Hall of Testimony," where they hand you a passport ID of a young person whose fate is updated as you move along. With your passport, you come to identify with a human story, a reminder of real suffering and injustice at the hands of other brothers and sisters. Following, the exhibit called "We the People" stands as a reminder that we are the people who by our own deeds or lack of involvement contribute to the pain, suffering, and injustice. Yet in the midst of all of this stand great testimonies of courage and hope. The words and wisdom of people like Anne Frank shine through, people whose faith and trust in God still lives on and beckons us to hold fast, even in the face of brokenness, fear, and death.

The guest book placed at the museum's exit contains one comment repeated over and over and over by visitors: "Will we allow this to happen again; will the cycle be repeated?" This question rises before us every day—from the areas of immigration reform, health care, and foreign policy to how we interact with those in our family and neighborhood. Will we let this happen again? Will we be silent, will we stand back, or will we take the risk to speak the truth in love? The choice is ours!

Our Hebrew scriptures give us the stories of great men and women—Ruth and Esther, Amos and Isaiah—who took great risk to speak the truth. They called for a new exodus, for right relationship. Their passion for justice made a difference not only in individual lives, but also in an entire people. We can walk through their Hall of Testimony, formed by scripture, and discover the fire of suffering and passion for justice that opened their lives to the living God.

Isaiah spoke to the heart of his people after a deeply moving experience of God. His encounter with God brought him in touch with his own sinfulness and need for purification. He sensed the enormous abyss between God's holiness and human frailty, and bemoaned the unclean lips of both himself and his people. Only a burning coal could purify his lips so that he could speak his response: "Here I am!" Only the fire of suffering could purify the people to re-enter God's covenant. Isaiah stood in the presence of the holiness of God and from this encounter, he accepted the commission to go forth and speak the word—a word alive with God's power, a word of both comfort and discomfort.

Like the people of the Hebrew scriptures, we have forgotten who we are as broken yet beloved daughters and sons of God, given responsibility to care for the earth and its creatures. We have forgotten our relationship with God and with the whole of creation. As the United Nations Environmental Sabbath prayer laments: "We have turned our backs on the cycles of life, we have sought only our own security, we have exploited simply for our own ends, we have abused our power, we have forgotten who we are." The prayer concludes with a plea for mercy: "We ask for forgiveness, we ask for the gift of remembering, we ask for the strength to change."

Conversion lies at the heart of the prophetic message. God desires to turn our forgetful hearts towards the Creator of life so that we do not perpetuate our suffering and death. Isaiah expresses the anguish of a loving God who sees how lost we are: "An ox knows its owner, and an ass, its master's manger; but Israel does not know, my people [have] not understood" (Is 1:3). The prophet calls for reflection on the wounds of the world: "Where would you yet be struck, you that rebel again and again? The whole head is sick, the whole heart faint" (Is 1:5). He invites the people instead to travel on a way toward healing, to "walk in the light of the

LORD" (Is 2:5). Isaiah calls the people to return, to make a path for the LORD; to embark on a new exodus. We the people repeat this journey today. With Isaiah's passion for justice—for right relationship—we heed the groans of the old, the poor, the hungry, the different, or the stranger instead of honoring only the rich, the strong, the young, and the successful. This draws us all toward the loving God in whom we find our deepest identity.

Believers today who read Isaiah's words take the prophet's vision to be both promise and challenge. Like the poets responsible for the Book of Consolation, we are convinced that Isaiah's hopes for change will find fulfillment; that a new exodus will occur. The Servant Song of Isaiah reminds us of our own role as servants: to bind up wounds, to be bearers of light, to open up new roads and highways. The song unfolds the challenge and promise for the servant: "Because of his affliction he shall see the light in fullness of days; through his suffering, my servant shall justify many, and their guilt he shall bear" (Is 53:11). To be a servant is not to anesthetize oneself to the pain of the world, but to live passionately and fully for the sake of others, knowing we are connected to those who have come before and those who will follow. As George Bernard Shaw writes, "Life is no brief candle to me. It is a sort of splendid torch which I have got a hold of for the moment, and I want to make it burn as brightly as possible before handing it on to future generations."

As religious educators, we must be bringers of God's light and justice; we must dare to be prophets and dare to be servants. We stand with the biblical prophet Amos and with Martin Luther King Jr., who echoed his words, declaring, "Let justice surge like water, and goodness like an unfailing stream" (Am 5:24). Isaiah calls us to do away with the clenched fist and the wicked word (we are reminded again of the caption "Words break more than bones"). We pause to check our actions and words. Do they rise up and empower, or do they bow down and enslave? Who is in and who is out of our circle of love, of relationships, of concern? The poet Edwin Markham writes:

> He drew a circle that shut me out—
> Heretic, rebel, a thing to flout.
> But love and I had the wit to win:
> We drew a circle that took him in!

The call, then, is to include the stranger, the poor, the rich, the weak, the strong. Love knows no barriers. A true servant is one who seeks to embody love, reaching out to embrace others in both their beauty and their agony. St. Augustine describes this well:

> Love has hands to help others,
> It has feet to hasten to aid of the poor
> and needy,
> It has eyes to see misery and want,
> It has ears to hear the sighs and sorrows
> of others,
> That's what love looks like.

The recompense for reaching out is great. Isaiah reminds us that if we spend ourselves in behalf of the hungry and satisfy the needs of the oppressed, our light will shine in the darkness and God will make us like refreshing springs of water in the desert. "Then you shall call, and the LORD will answer, you shall cry for help, and he will say: 'Here I am!'" (Is 58:9).

And so we are invited to be open, vulnerable, sensitive, and willing to lay down our lives. But where does this strength come from? It comes in the gift of God's self to us. Like Isaiah, we must stand in the presence of the Lord, and in the power of this relationship be sent forth. If the church is to be prophetic, vital, and holy, not merely socially enlightened, we must recover this deep and transforming spirituality.

It is time to dip into the well of truth and love from which the mystics and saints drew their energy. Our words will only have authority if they are steeped in the word of God in response to contemporary needs. Millions of people all over the earth are aching for peace, justice, and safe environments. The earth itself is in travail. Yet we believe that the capacity for healing is astounding. It is at work in nature, history, relationships, and in our own hearts. We engage in the process of healing even as we bear the pain. We may not be asked for the supreme sacrifice of our lives, but we are asked to look at life with the eyes of Christ who points the way to justice and integrity. We are always in need of encouragement to keep going in spite of the obstacles. We can never take victory for granted, but we live in expectation and hope.

We are challenged to live in the spirit of resurrection and to believe that we are part of a great circle of life on earth. We are not separate little beings; we are connected, and we do have responsibility. We are the body of Christ!

And so, we are all confronted with the challenge to do justice, to love, to forgive, to invite. In other words, we strive to live as Christ lived, as one in the Spirit. Walter Burghardt encourages us in our struggle to live this truth:

> Think big, love large. Press the powerful on the hill to humanize our horrifying housing, to crush the drug empire at its source, to bring the warring to peace tables, to treat refugees like people and not political footballs, to reverence the earth before it rises to destroy us. But think small as well, love little. I mean, let your head, your hand, your heart go out to one man, one woman, one child who desperately needs what you have to give. It's Jesus all over again. While saving a world, he still had time for individuals.

Let us pray that our eyes, ears, tongues, hearts, and minds will catch the fire of justice. And that while striving to save the many, we, too, will have time for the one, the stranger, the lost, and the alone, and become one in the house of God!

12

GOD'S LIBERATING POWER

We have only begun
to imagine the fullness of life
How could we tire of hope?

Denise Levertov

Inside each of us there is a wonderful desire for freedom. But there is also an inclination toward the selfishness that is ultimately a form of enslavement. Even though every human being is constantly being drawn to God, there are spaces within our hearts where we still do not believe in God's liberating power. These are the places where we must confront our demons.

The Gospel of Mark brings us face to face with "The Gerasene Demoniac" (5:1–21), a man so possessed by evil spirits that their name is Legion, for there are many of them. He wanders among the tombs on a hillside, "always crying out and bruising himself with stones." He shouts out at the top of his voice, "What have you to do with me, Jesus, Son of the Most High God?" Yet

Jesus overpowers the demons who hold him captive and the man "pleaded to remain with him."

What are our demons? What are the forces within us that cause us to be self-destructive, that alienate us from Jesus? Our demons can be expectations, both our own and others that fracture relationships and pressure us to prove our worth. They can be the loneliness and alienation that we experience coming from a lack of intimacy with ourselves. We are always on the move, in a hurry, and so we often lack intimacy with ourselves, others, and God. This isolation, coupled with the fear of disclosure, often keeps us bound and cornered in the very space that we should feel free to move around in.

Our demons can be the fears and anxieties that get in our way. Hurts from the past leave us unsure whether we can trust the future, whether we can forgive and forget or will go on nursing a grudge.

The demon of control and manipulation is alive and well in our relationships. It shows up in the ways we relate to others as objects, always attempting to give ourselves a sense of purpose and value. The demon of control is at work in our desire to possess, to smother others' hopes with our agendas. We experience this same pull in our inability to forgive, to reconcile, to let go of negativity and resentment that can eat away at us.

Sometimes the demons that bind us come from the unhealthy guilt that we carry, the "shoulds," the "I wishes," the regrets and preoccupations with the past; the inability to laugh at ourselves, to take ourselves seriously, but with a light touch—this, too, can be a demon.

Thomas Merton was keenly aware of the power of these demons and the ways in which they can lead us to a loss of soul. With a prophet's eye, Merton saw how Western civilization embraces the image of the false self with all its addictions to power, money, and violence. In such a society, he saw human beings live empty, alienated lives, disconnected from the true source of their beings.

To grow into our true selves, to be liberated from the demons that plague us, we must learn to let go. The possessed man was fearful and yet trusted that Jesus would break the chains and set him free. We, too, must let go of who we have been so as to live more fully. St. Teresa of Avila says that it doesn't matter whether we are held down by a string or a rope; the reality is that we still cannot fly. What is keeping us from flying with the strength of God's liberating power?

Walter Burghardt writes,

> Whether it's turning twenty-one, forty, or sixty-five, whether it's losing your health or your hair, your looks or your beauty, your money or your memory, a person you love or a possession you prize, yesterday's rapture or today's applause, you have to move on. Essential to the human's pilgrimage to the Christian journey is the self-emptying more or less like Christ's own emptying. Time and again, from womb to tomb, you have to let go. And to let go is to die a little. It's painful, it can be bloody; and so we hang [on], clutch our yesterdays, like Linus's blanket, refuse to grow.

This clinging, this refusal to let go will not do, especially for we who call ourselves Christian. We are called to follow in the traces of the one who emptied himself to become one with us, who let go of his beloved mother, his friends and family, who let go of the very gift of life. Learning to let go rather than to hold on tightly is key.

Anthony DeMello writes:

> Whatever you treasure,
> must be held in the hollow of your hand
> as water is held
> clutch at it and it is gone,
> appropriate it to yourself and you soil it,
> set it free and it is forever yours.

When we look into our lives and think of moments when we truly opened our hearts, or dispossessed ourselves, what do we find? Riches in abundance—we die a little to live more richly.

The journey of the human heart is a journey of liberation from slavery to freedom. We are challenged to name the demons of our lives. Often, we gain power over our darkness by naming it. Jesus named the demons and they quieted down. A strength and serenity comes from trying to embrace and gain control over these limitations and fears. As we confront them, we begin to imagine a new path; we release our minds from mental debates, and energies begin to flow. It is the process of conversion.

One discovers the life of the true self by sinking into the present. We come home to ourselves and know the place as if for the first time. Home is the place where we can be ourselves, accept ourselves, and love ourselves, warts and all. Ultimately, home is the place of solitude. As we come home, our God runs to meet us, embrace us, and bring us back to life. In solitude, our masks are burned and we are made free to celebrate our blessedness and our brokenness.

Jesus' resurrection is what gives us hope that we can be freed from all that binds, enslaves, and destroys. It is a sign of liberation that promises that with God's grace, we can move beyond the many little deaths we endure. It is a challenge that encourages us to allow the Spirit of the risen Lord to shape our thinking, acting, and way of being.

The glory of the resurrection points to a radical trust in God—when everything seemed to be falling apart, Jesus stepped in and turned everything around, just as he did to the man possessed by the demon. Not only did he free him from the clutches of evil, but he also sent him to bear witness and call others into this freedom. And the story is repeated in our lives. It is with our newfound freedom that we are called to bear witness and minister to others, especially those around us who are lonely in need of companionship, bruised in need of healing, lost in need of anchoring, or discouraged in need of hope.

Through faith we know that we are the body of Christ and Christ constantly yearns to be born again in every human heart. Will we be part of that birth and set the Spirit free in lives, opening the doors to let the enemy stomp out? If the reign of God and the praxis of Jesus truly inspire our ministry, we will always remember that religious education is not about indoctrinating and controlling people, it is about freeing them from their fear and alienations. It is about facilitating their personal encounter with God so that they can live to the full in the liberating joy of the kingdom.

Let us remember the paths we have taken thus far—paths that have, at times, enslaved us. We lament our failures, our blindness, our holding on to our demons, and yet we are confident and move forward in hope and trust. Our hope is not in ourselves, but in the transforming fire of God's love. Let us carry with us this powerful image of Cyril of Jerusalem, the fourth-century theologian who wrote:

> If fire passing through a mass of iron makes the whole of it glow, so that what was cold becomes burning, and what was black is made bright, so too, the power of the Spirit transforms our minds, and indeed the clay of

creation itself, so that what was cold and dark
becomes bright and glowing.

We, like Jesus, are sent to call one another forth with the Spirit of God, the voice of God, to set others free to live the resurrection now. This is our call and responsibility. As we continue our
journey, let us be about God's liberating power!

13

((∞))

BEARER OF HOPE, RESTORING SPIRIT

Put your hope in God,
be stouthearted, put your hope in God.

Psalm 43:5

Hope is always in season, for the experience of uncertainty in our church and in our world is always with us. With watchful eyes and compassionate hearts, we cannot avoid noting signs of discouragement, even disillusionment, all around us. The media continually flashes before us the faces of the oppressed and suffering. The struggles of these times would be unbearable without the promise of our rich tradition.

Do we dare to remember the whispers of hope, the message of courage? Do we accept the challenge that Christopher Fry expresses so well in his poem "A Sleep of Prisoners":

> Thank God our time is now,
> when wrong comes up to face us everywhere
> Never to leave us till we take,

The longest stride of soul men ever took.
Affairs are now soul size.
The enterprise
Is exploration into God.

Affairs, indeed, are now soul size! We know that hope is not the naive expectation that all will go effortlessly and according to plan, that anguish will remain a stranger. Rather, hope is remembering. It is aptly symbolized by an anchor. The Letter to the Hebrews proclaims that hope is the sure and steadfast "anchor of the soul" (Heb 6:19) that steadies us. It enables us to draw strength from God's presence and power in history, and in our world today.

The enterprise is nothing less than an exploration into God, the God of Hope. It is, as Walt Whitman described, a journey into the deep:

Sail forth—steer for the deep waters only,
Reckless O soul, exploring, I with thee, and
    thou with me,
For we are bound where mariner has not yet
    dared to go,
And we will risk the ship, ourselves and all.
O my brave Soul!
O farther, farther sail!

Hoping against hope, Abraham believed and thus became the leader of many nations. Women such as Sarah, Rebecca, and Deborah kept alive the hope of Israel's restoration. Leaning on this rich tradition and the memory of men and women who hoped frantically and were not disappointed, we stretch out to be bearers of this hope: to love, to heal, to challenge, to build up. We risk the ship, ourselves and all, even when our circumstances seem almost hopeless, because we learn that these limited moments are really experiences of grace—a gift in disguise. They call us to integrity and signal us to walk in truth and humility, espousing a way of life that can embrace both joy and sorrow.

Through our grief, God reaches deeply into our hearts and touches us with his healing balm, and we become like rivers of living water, springing up renewed, made whole again, and eager to help renew the spirits of others. Our triumph over pain is not that we can avoid it, but that we can find meaning in it, integrate it, and allow it to draw us closer to our God.

In that depth of connection with the font of life lies our hope. We are made new and become bigger than the challenges we face. Worry ends where hope in God begins. The issues we face can be huge, but they are never as huge as God. "Therefore, we are not discouraged; rather, although our outer self is wasting away, our inner self is being renewed day by day" (2 Cor 4:16).

Our hope is that God will give us the wisdom to become the best, life-giving, hopeful people that we can become, rooted in God and held firm by the faith we possess. For in the presence of an awakened spirit, problems fade and strength is restored.

The resurrection of Jesus is witness to God's triumph over pain and death. Because of the resurrection we can hope that we, too, will rise again; that everything dark will turn to light. We must never forget that God's harmony reigns supreme. Even when we do not experience God's light, it is always our hope. Indeed, to be alive and vital is to believe that the golden flowers of God are in bud, that there is still the invitation to grow and nurture hearts. Denise Levertov spurs us to imagine fullness of life:

> We have only begun
> To imagine the fullness of life
> How could we tire of hope?
> —so much is in bud.

So much is in bud, and our hope in God is not only an expectation for change to happen in the world, but for change to happen in us.

We are summoned to imagine that things can be different, better, and more wholesome. Like Jesus, we must embrace the darkness and know that escape from bondage comes when we hug our dragons and realize with David Whyte "that anything that does not bring you alive is too small for you."

We are still learning that when we trust and let go, our vision expands and we see the whole for the first time in our lives.

> A pilgrim was walking along a road when one day he passed what seemed to be a monk sitting in the field. Nearby, men were working on a stone building.
> "You look like a monk," the pilgrim said.
> "I am that," said the monk.
> "Who is that working on the abbey?"
> "My monks," said the man. "I am the abbot."
> "Oh! That's wonderful," the pilgrim said. "It's so good to see a monastery going up."
> "We're tearing it down!" the abbot said.
> "Tearing it down!" the pilgrim cries. "Whatever for?"
> "So we can see the sun rise at dawn," the abbot said.

To lose something is often to renew it. We have lost much in the course of our lives, and yet we believe that in the losing there is finding. Hope sharpens our spirit and, consequently, our creativity and initiative. In the words of Pope Paul VI, "Our church needs her perennial Pentecost, she needs need fire in the heart, words on her lips, and a glance that is prophetic."

We need that same fire in the heart. Paul reminds Timothy to "stir into a flame the gift of God" (2 Tm 1:6). Like Timothy, we must get in touch with the power of the Spirit at the center of our lives and communities, and experience God's presence lighting up our drooping spirits. Out of this fortifying experience we embrace the fire, the passion to go forth, to bring the vision of the gospel into every strata of society, and to engage the community.

With fire in our hearts, the words that flow from our lips become a source of hope and a challenge. All of us who catechize retell the story and pass on the incredible good news of Jesus, the one who restores and makes all things new. In this endeavor, we have much to learn from Jesus' unique teaching style. He had a special way of inviting people to reflect on their lives and to see with fresh eyes.

This same Jesus beckons us to proclaim the word and draw the discouraged, dispirited, and even nonbelievers to God's truth. With words on the lips and prophecy in the core of our being, we are compelled to direct the power of the Spirit's fiery blaze to the shadowy areas of human existence, to those who struggle under discriminatory systems, to those who walk in the shadow of war, to those who make decisions about war and peace.

Hope is the driving force in all things new. It is the capacity to dream the future and instigate many acts of communion, collaboration, joint ventures, and munificent efforts. Edmund Burke famously wrote, " The only thing necessary for the triumph of evil is for enough good people to do nothing." And so, we are called to do something.

We are called to work together in our communities and see the interconnectedness of all. It is the whole community that catechizes with its rituals, faith formation efforts, liturgies, gatherings, and celebrations.

In fact, the parish is the curriculum and all must be bearers of hope, restorers of spirit.

The evangelical preacher Vance Havner once commented, "Christians, like snowflakes, are frail, but when they stick together they can stop traffic." If we stick together, we can build a stronger, more authentic church, a church that labors to bring healing to fractured relationships while embracing truth and right relationship. Then, we will not be afraid to embrace the responsibility that comes with power, while rejecting its abuse wherever we find it. Then, we will be a church that empowers and supports lay and ordained ministers while confronting clericalism. We will be a church that welcomes new thinking and new ways of being authentic as a people of faith. We will be a faithful people of God drawing from a wonderfully rich tradition while rejecting the politics of fear and divisiveness that can be so crippling of mind, heart, and vision. Together, we can be so much more than our individual fears. Collectively, we form one body of Christ, and are enlivened and empowered by the circle of love that is the Triune God.

Consider a circle as a paradigm of hope. In the circle, we do not experience one person *over* another, one strength *dominating* another. Rather, in the circle we affirm our distinctiveness and seek to respect one another's gifts. As one, we give collective voice to the power of the gospel of Jesus. In *his* Spirit, we pledge to be a voice for the oppressed, to pay attention to the needy, and to stand in solidarity with the poor. We are witness to gospel justice. We attend to the work of transformation.

Understanding the world in the light of hope means to endure in faith; waiting, as in winter, for the certain fertility of the earth, the coming of the harvest of plenty. As we strive to heal and think anew, we must recall that God does not leave us orphans and that the Spirit is moving among us always. We must stand on that assurance, knowing that while affairs are soul size, the enterprise is still an exploration into God in whom we will become bearers of hope and restorers of spirit.

14

LOVE UNFOLDING, IGNITING OUR YES

Oh, hear Him within you speaking this infinite love. . .
lifting the sky of the soul with the expansions of light,
shaping new heights and new depths. . . .

Jessica Powers

Love is at the heart of all creation. It continues to unfold, drawing us ever more profoundly into the embrace of a lavish God.
This wondrous relationship, this love unbounded, deepens and
develops over time. It grows through seasons of dark and light,
always nudging us to remember and hold fast to God's promise of
faithfulness—his covenant.

Love unfolding is the way of Jesus. He called his disciples to
"come and see." Now he is calling us into deeper friendship and
interconnection with him and with all of life. This bond of one-
ness, this fastening of the spirit to God, sustains us on the path.

It generates and ignites a fresh energy and propels us to give voice to our yes anew.

This unfolding love has a long history. It has a long past, yet it is an ever-present reality. It is the love that enfolds all of creation and sets a rainbow in the sky as a reminder of the steadfastness of God's covenant. It is the generosity of God encountered in the generosity of Jesus. It is the love of God that, in the words of e.e. cummings, is "walking inside the ragged edges of our souls," drawing us to wholeness.

The treasures of love unfolding are found in the word of God. Psalm 119 reminds us "The unfolding of your word gives light, it imparts understanding." As catechetical leaders we are privileged to prepare the soil so that all can come to experience this showing of God's love. Our ministry is to help unfold the treasures of this word and invite the whole community into a fresh encounter with Jesus.

St. Amadeus, in the twelfth century, offered this reflection:

> Lord, we have heard your word, and we have been astounded. We have pondered your marvels and we have fainted. As your word descended, our hearts have been melted. . . . You shed light in the darkness, dew upon dryness, and in the bitter frost, you kindled a raging fire.

"You kindled a raging fire." This is the hope that we must learn to unfold. And it is the hope that we must hold onto as we come face to face with the sharp edges of our world today and the fear of what might be looming ahead. Precisely in these times we must beg God to kindle a raging fire in our darkness and enfold us in strengthening love—to face tomorrow, to set out without a map, to endure with the knowledge that fear can never prevail against God's word.

In his book, *Begin with the Heart: Recovering a Sacramental Vision*, Daniel O'Leary reflects on this unfolding love and suggests that "God walks in two shoes—the shoe of creation and the shoe of incarnation." Throughout the centuries, the poets and artists have observed that the beauty and gift of the natural world reveal the glory and power of God, and that earth itself cries out in praise of her maker. "Earth with her thousand voices, praise God," says Samuel Taylor Coleridge.

O'Leary points out that, "It takes immense imagination to take the incarnation literally, to identify God's signature on everything around us, to see God's face behind every face, to identify and appreciate the Lover-God who comes to us disguised as our lives."

I recall an encounter I had with the face of God early one morning. A homeless man on the streets of Hollywood stopped to talk and tell me that he was so thankful to wake up and not feel cold, even though he had slept on the streets under a cardboard roof. In the midst of his seeming hardship and impoverishment he was still filled with gratitude for this simple gift of warmth that most of us take for granted.

As I reflected on this encounter, I knew that I was privileged to experience love unfolding in this man's gracious and positive attitude. He surely bore witness to the words of Etty Hillesum," You are God in hiding, you are the cluttered house that hides the Holy One." The Holy One hidden and now revealed in the homeless.

As Catholics, we live in the realm of the sacraments. We are called to a sacramental consciousness, to notice, to see more. There is a story told of a master who lay dying. A disciple begged him, for their sakes, not to go. "But if I do not go," the master said, "how will you ever see?" "What are we not seeing that we can see when you are gone?" the disciple pressed. And the spiritual master said, "All that I ever did was sit at the river bank handing out river water. After I am gone I trust you will notice the river."

The task of the catechetical minister is not only about passing on new information, but also to keep the eyes and the ears of learners open to notice the many unfoldings, the river of love, the presence of God who comes as stranger and friend.

John O'Donohue suggests that "the imagination is like a lantern, it illuminates the inner landscape of our lives." He goes on to lament that there are people who only see dullness in the world and that is because our looking has become repetitive and blind. There is a danger to that kind of dullness. Blindness or loss of courage can dampen spirits, press us down. But we remember that God walks not only in the two shoes of creation and incarnation, but also that hope springs from God's gracious hands, from word and Spirit. The memory and stories of our saving history assure us that God is with us through it all, leading and drawing us to wholeness. "I will never forget you. . . . upon the palms of my hands I have written your name" (Is 49:15–16).

Enlivened by the power of the Spirit, we keep moving, though the pace is slow—moving through the dark, fueled by hope. Teilhard de Chardin writes, "In all these dark moments, O God, grant that I may understand that it is you who are painfully parting the fibers of my being in order to penetrate the very marrow of my substance."

The daily disappointments and struggles that "knock, blow, and burn" as the poet John Donne puts it, help shape us anew. They make space and give us compassion for the struggles of others.

Indeed, the stripping of our ability to share material gifts with one another can connect us in new ways to God as we look for permanent and lasting gifts that we can give and receive. The dead ends, the current crisis—whatever it may be—ironically have the potential to become the very means of lifting us to new horizons, new wisdom, and discernment as they shake us up to re-examine how we live our lives.

It is possible to have a new kind of world, a world where there will be more caring, more thought for others, more laughter and joy, more sharing of resources; but we must be willing to make the changes in our lifestyles and practices that will ensure a better place for all. Only then will the world orient toward healing and away from destruction. Such a world is linked in kindness and responsibility for the other.

> All things by immortal power
> To each other linked are.
> That thou canst not stir a flower
> Without troubling a star.
> —Francis Thompson

God is not finished with creation. We are called upon to do our bit in completing the enterprise. God calls us to cooperate with his Spirit, who creates a new time in which love is not greedy or self-seeking, but truly faithful and genuinely free, open to others, respectful of their dignity, seeking their good, radiating joy and beauty.

God having first said yes to us by birthing us into life, then creating and redeeming us, now challenges us to say yes and open our hearts so that God can ignite us, set us on fire, work through us for the life of the world and the growth of the body of Christ.

The unfolding of God's mercy and forgiveness will never happen without our cooperation and support. If we choose to stay locked up in our own little world, in our bubble, then we and our world will smother, lose our breath.

> Life is either a daring adventure or nothing.
> To keep our faces toward change
> And behave like free spirits

> In the presence of fate
> Is strength undefeatable.
>
> —Helen Keller

Will we model strength undefeatable? Do we know that the way that we preach and evangelize reflects the condition of our own hearts and spirits? Will we let our rootedness in Christ unfold the gift of grace and blessing at the heart of our own lives and ministry?

The igniting of our yes will, at times, bring us face to face with our own vulnerability. There will be times when we won't be able to respond to the many needs all around us; we won't have all the words. Our yes may lack energy and spark. Yet we sorely know that while one person lacks dignity, while human practices of pollution ravish the earth, our yes is not yet ignited. We know that while attitudes and relationships that diminish the well-being of others still exist, while people are still used and abused, our yes is not yet ignited. We know that when a poor homeless man is doused with gasoline and set on fire in the streets of Los Angeles, our yes is not yet ignited. And while we continue to be consumers and amass for ourselves rather than disciples, our yes is not yet ignited.

In spite of our covenant breaking, we are beckoned to keep pleading for the courage to ignite our yes: yes to participating in the struggle for human dignity for all of God's people, yes to being involved in creating a world of harmony, peace, justice, care for the earth. Indeed, we must allow the proclamation that Christ is alive to so consume us that our hearts will be on fire with the fire of God.

Our challenge is to keep alive a sturdy appreciation of God's lavish love; to be, more than ever, aware of Christ in ourselves and one another; to keep his passion in front of us; to trust deeply, never succumbing to the angst and pessimism that at times sweeps across hearts and pries them off center.

The great illusion of leadership is to think that people can be guided out of the desert, out of darkness, by those who have never tasted or experienced pain. The bleakness and emptiness of the past or present can never be filled or healed without willingness to enter into the journey with another and to find in the companion of suffering the way to freedom and peace. This perspective influences the way we live, giving a new meaning to love. The way of Jesus was the way of the cross, and it is often our way as well. But it is a cross steeped in resurrection's promise, in love unfolding.

There is a story about a medieval monk who announced to his congregation that the next Sunday evening he would be preaching on the love of God. As the shadows fell and the light ceased to come in through the cathedral windows on that Sunday night, the congregation gathered for the sermon. In the darkness of the altar, the monk lit a candle and carried it to the crucifix. As he stood in silence and illuminated this sign of love poured out, a hush fell on the congregation. There was nothing else to say about the love of God.

Anything other than a loving relationship with God leaves us empty, lonely, and unfulfilled. John Cassian, the early church father, suggests: "Each hour, every moment, we need to keep opening up the ground of our heart with the plough of the gospel." This encounter with a love that breaks open the clay of our hearts purifies, frees, and allows us to become truly ourselves.

We know that we are made for God, that there is a God-shaped hole in all of us that only God can fill. Something inside of us bleeds toward God, as Dorothy Walters proposes when she writes:

> Something inside me,
> Constantly bleeds toward God.

That's why I keep writing.
Slipping messages under the door.

Let us take the time to be still, to experience the unfolding love of God in the very fabric of our lives, in our prayer, and in our work. When we do, the days and hours of our lives become lit from above. Fear and anxiety are cast from our world. The love at the heart of all creation draws us ever more profoundly into the embrace of our lavish God.

SOURCES

Angelou, Maya. *And Still I Rise*. New York: Random House, 1978.

Bailie, Gil. *Violence Unveiled: Humanity at the Crossroads*. New York: Crossroad Publishing Company, 1996.

Benshea, Noah. *Jacob the Baker: Gentle Wisdom for a Complicated World*. New York: Ballantine Books, 1990.

Bernardin, Cardinal Joseph. *Catholic Common Ground Initiative: Foundational Documents*. New York: Crossroad Publishing Company, 1997.

Blake, William. *The Complete Poems*. Edited by Alicia Ostriker. New York: Penguin Classics, 1988.

Bonhoeffer, Dietrich. *The Cost of Discipleship*. New York: Simon & Schuster, 1995.

Bowes, George Seaton. *Illustrative Gatherings for Teachers and Preachers*. Whitefish, MT: Kessinger Publishing, LLC, 2008.

Browning, Elizabeth Barrett. *Aurora Leigh, Book VII*.

Burgess, Ruth and Kathy Galloway, eds. *Praying for the Dawn: A Resource Book for the Ministry of Healing*. Glasgow, Scotland: Wildgoose Publications, 2007.

Burghardt, Walter J. *Dare to Be Christ*. New York: Paulist Press, 1991.

———. *Lovely Eyes Not His*. New York: Paulist Press, 1988.

Burns, Robert. *Poems and Songs of Robert Burns.* Edited by Andrew Lang. London, England: Methuen & Co., Ltd., 1926.

Catherine of Genoa, St. *Treatise on Purgatory.* Indianapolis, IN: Ex Fontibus Co., 2007.

de Chardin, Pierre Teilhard. *Pierre Teilhard de Chardin: Writings.* Maryknoll, NY: Orbis Books, 1999.

De Mello, Anthony. *The Heart of the Enlightened.* New York: Image, 1997.

Delp, Alfred. *Prison Writings.* Maryknoll, NY: Orbis Books, 2004.

Dickinson, Emily. "If I Can Stop One Heart from Breaking." *Selected Poems of Dickinson.* Hertfordshire, England: Wordsworth Editions, Ltd., 1998.

Dillard, Annie. *Pilgrim at Tinker Creek.* New York: Harper Perennial Modern Classics, 2007.

Donne, John. *Collected Poems of John Donne.* Hertfordshire, England: Wordsworth Editions, Ltd., 1999.

Dumas, Alexandre. *The Count of Monte Cristo.* New York: Penguin Classics, 2003.

Foster, Richard. *Prayer: Finding the Heart's True Home.* San Francisco: HarperOne, 1992.

Frank, Anne. *Anne Frank – The Diary of a Young Girl.* New York: Pocket Books, 1969.

Fry, Christopher. *A Sleep of Prisoners.* New York: Oxford University Press, 1951.

Glassé, Cyril. *The New Encyclopedia of Islam.* Lanham, MD: Rowman & Littlefield Publishers, Inc., 2008.

Greave, Peter. *The Seventh Gate.* Albuquerque, NM: Transatlantic Arts, 1978.

Hafiz. *The Gift.* Translated by Daniel Landinsky. New York: Penguin Non-Classics, 1999.

Hart, Columba. *Hildegard of Bingen: Scivias,* translated by Jane Bishop. New York: Paulist Press, 1990.

Havner, Vance. In *The Purpose Driven Life,* by Rick Warren, Grand Rapids, MI: Zondervan, 2002.

Heaney, Seamus. *The Cure of Troy.* Dublin, Ireland: Field Day, 1990.

Hopkins, Gerard Manley. "God's Grandeur" *Norton Anthology of Poetry.* Edited by Margaret Ferguson, Mary Jo Salter, and Jonathan Stallworthy. New York: W.W. Norton & Company, Inc., 2005.

Hillesum, Etty. *An Interrupted Life: The Diaries of Etty Hillesum.* New York: Pocket Books, 1991.

Hubbard, Howard. *I Am Bread Broken: A Spirituality for the Catechist.* New York: Crossroad/Faith & Formation, 1996.

Ilibagiza, Immaculée. *Left to Tell: Discovering God Amidst the Rwandan Holocaust.* New York: Hay House, 2007.

Juliana of Norwich. *Revelations of Divine Love,* translated by M.L del Mastro. New York: Image Books, Division of Doubleday, Inc. 1977.

Keller, Helen. *Story of My Life.* New York: Dover Publications, 1996.

Kennelly, Brendan. *Familiar Strangers: New and Selected Poems 1960–2004.* Northumberland, England: Bloodaxe Books, Ltd., 2004.

———. *A Time for Voices Selected Poems.* Northumberland, England: Bloodaxe Books, Ltd., 2004.

Kushner, Harold. "God's Fingerprints on the Soul" in *Handbook for the Soul,* Edited by Richard Carlson and Benjamin Shield. Boston: Little, Brown and Company, 1996.

Levertov, Denise. *Selected Poems.* New York: New Directions Book, 2002.

Livingston, Patricia. *Let In the Light: Facing the Hard Stuff with Hope.* Notre Dame, IN: Ave Maria Press, 2006.

Los Angeles Times, October 5, 2000.

Machado, Antonio. quoted in *Ten Poems to Change Your Life.* Edited by Roger Housden. New York: Harmony, 2001.

Mandela, Nelson. 1994 May. Inaugural Address. Retrieved on 2009 June at: http://www.africa.upenn.edu/Articles_Gen/Inaugural_Speech_17984.html.

————. *A Long Walk to Freedom: The Autobiography of Nelson Mandela.* Newport Beach, CA: Back Bay Books, Inc., 1995.

Martel, Yann. *Life of Pi.* New York: Harcourt, Inc., 2001.

Markham, Edwin. *The Shoes of Happiness and Other Poems.* New York: Double Day Page, 1915.

————. "How the Great Guest Came." *Book of Jesus.* Edited by Calvin Miller. New York: Touchstone, 1998.

Merton, Thomas. "Letter to a Young Activist." *Thomas Merton: Essential Writings.* Edited by Christine M. Bochen. Maryknoll, NY: Orbis Books, 2000.

————. *Thoughts in Solitude.* New York: Farrar, Straus and Giroux, 1958.

O'Donohue, John. *Divine Beauty: The Invisible Embrace.* New York: Bantam Press, 2003.

O'Leary, Daniel. *Begin with the Heart: Recovering a Sacramental Vision.* Dublin: Columba Press, 2008.

Oliver, Mary. *New and Selected Poems*. Boston: Beacon Press, 1992.

———. *Why I Wake Early*. Boston: Beacon Press, 2004.

———. *Thirst*. Boston: Beacon Press, 2000.

Owen, Wilfred. *The War Poems of Wilfred Owen*. Edited by John Silkin. Vauxhall Bridge Road, London: Sinclair-Stevenson, Ltd., 1994.

Powers, Jessica. *Selected Poetry of Jessica Powers*. Edited by Robert Morneau and Regina Siegfried. Kansas City, MO: Sheed & Ward, 1996.

Quindlen, Anna. *A Short Guide to a Happy Life*. New York: Random House, 2000.

Religious Sisters of Charity, Mission in Companionship Document, General Chapter, 2001.

Rilke, Rainer Maria. *Rilke's Book of Hours: Love Poems to God*. Translated by Anita Barrows and Johanna Macy. New York: Riverhead Books, 1996.

Rupp, Joyce. *The Star in My Heart*. Philadelphia: Innisfree Press, 1990.

Siegel, Bernie. "Love: The Work of the Soul," *Handbook for the Soul*. Edited by Richard Carlson and Benjamin Shield. Boston: Little, Brown and Company, 1996.

Tagore, Rabindranath. *The Gardener*. Whitefish, MT: Kessinger Publishing L.K.C., 2004.

Thompson, Francis. *Complete Poetical Works of Francis Thompson*. Brookfield, CT: Roaring Brooks Press, 2007.

Wallington, David. *The Secret Room: Story of Corrie ten Boom*. Norwich, England: Religious and Moral Education Press, 1981.

Walters, Dorothy. *Marrows of Flame: Poems of the Spiritual Journey*. Prescott, AZ: Hohm Press, 2000.

Whitman, Walter. *Passage to India.* Amsterdam, The Netherlands: Fredonia Books, 2004.

Whyte, David. *The House of Belonging.* Langley, WA: Many Rivers Press, 1998.

Wiesel, Elie. *Night.* New York: Bantam Books, 1982.

ADDITIONAL ACKNOWLEDGMENTS

(continued from page iv.)

"My Brilliant Image" by Hafiz is reprinted from the Penguin publication *I Heard God Laughing: Poems of Hope and Joy* by Daniel Ladinsky. Copyright © 1996 & 2006, Daniel Ladinsky and used with his permission.

"Beginners" is reprinted from *Candles in Babylon,* copyright ©1982 by Denise Levertov. Used by permission of New Directions Publishing Corp.

"The Avowal" is reprinted from *The Stream and the Sapphire,* copyright ©1984 by Denise Levertov. Used by permission of New Directions Publishing Corp.

"Doxology," "Come, South Wind," "The Little Nation," "The Mercy of God" and "This Is a Beautiful Time" are reprinted from *The Selected Poetry of Jessica Powers,* copyright © 1999, edited by Regina Siegfried and Robert F. Morneau. Published by ICS Publications, Washington D.C. All copyrights, Carmelite Monastery, Pewaukee, WI. Used with permission.

"A Sleep of Prisoners" by Christopher Fry is reprinted from his play, *A Sleep of Prisoners,* copyright © 1953 by Christopher Fry.

Edith Prendergast, R.S.C., is a member of the Religious Sisters of Charity and has been the director of the Office of Religious Education in the Catholic Archdiocese of Los Angeles since 1987. She is the beloved director of the archdiocese's annual Religious Education Congress—an event that attracts over forty thousand participants from around the world. Prendergast has served on the board of directors for the National Conference for Catechetical Leadership and has published articles in *Religion Teacher's Journal* and *Living with Christ*.

Founded in 1865, Ave Maria Press,
a ministry of the Congregation of
Holy Cross, is a Catholic publishing
company that serves the spiritual and
formative needs of the Church and its
schools, institutions, and ministers;
Christian individuals and families; and
others seeking spiritual nourishment.

For a complete listing of titles from

Ave Maria Press

Sorin Books

Forest of Peace

Christian Classics

visit www.avemariapress.com

ave maria press® / Notre Dame, IN 46556
A Ministry of the Indiana Province of Holy Cross